The Path
FORWARD

SURVIVING the NARCISSIST

Dedicated

To the amazing moderators and supportive members of our on-line community at www.ThePathForwardNow.com. You inspire me every day with your strength and heartfelt compassion for one another. No one understands what it is like to try to love a narcissist unless they have been through it firsthand. Together, we support one another on a level no one else can. Together, we will find a Path Forward!

TABLE OF CONTENTS

Introduction   1

The Path Forward   5

Chapter 1 – Understand It   7

What is narcissistic personality disorder?   13

Why do they devalue & discard us?   14

Why can't they change?   18

Why must we get real to heal?   20

Why do they seek out relationships?   22

What is the ego-self?   23

Why can't it ever work?   25

Why can't they love?   26

Why can't they accept love?   27

Why do they dread intimacy?   28

How do they brainwash us?   31

What are they like with children?   33

Why are we drawn to them?   34

Do they miss us?   36

Why do they keep coming back?   37

Why is it so hard for us to stay away?   38

Chapter 2 – Get It Out   43

Share Your Story   46

The Importance of Feeling   48

Letter to the Narcissist   53

Letter from the Narcissist   53

Chapter 3 – No Contact   55

Cognitive Dissonance   59

Obsessive Thoughts   64

Post-Traumatic Stress Disorder   66

Hoovering   69

NarcSpeak   70

Selective Memory   78

Chapter 4 – Get Real   81

Anger   82

Fear   88

Acceptance   93

Chapter 5 – Wake Up   99

Find Your Spirituality   104

The Power of Your Mind   107

Take Back Control 109

Retrain Your Brain 111

Manage Obsessive Thoughts 112

Thought Replacement 118

Positive Thinking 122

Create 124

Exercise 124

Music 125

Breathing Techniques 127

Meditation 127

Massage 129

Connect with Others 129

Give Back to Others 129

Celebrate Your Success 130

Chapter 6 – Heal 133

Forgiveness Letter 136

Live in the Moment 136

Travel 137

Gratitude List 138

Savor the Simplicities 139

Have a Love Affair with Yourself 139

The Hidden Benefits of Struggle 141

Moving Forward 142

Summary of Writing Assignments 145

Notes 146

About the Author   **147**

The Path Forward Coaching   **148**

Introduction

Have you suddenly found yourself in a relationship with someone who no longer understands you?

Someone you no longer understand?

In the beginning was he too good to be true? A prince in shining armour, who later turned critical, demeaning and even cruel? Does everything seem to be ALL ABOUT HIM? Is he insensitive to your needs, unappreciative of your input and indifferent to your feelings? Does he fail to recognize your giving, kind and thoughtful ways?

Do you feel as though you can do nothing right in his eyes? Are you constantly made to feel guilty when you have done nothing wrong? Do you feel like your relationship with him has become an emotional roller coaster ride you can't get off? Incredible highs one moment, followed by unbelievable lows the next?

Is he hot and then cold? Does he become distant and silent only to revert back by showering you with love and affection? Do you ever wonder if he has someone else? Is your gut telling you something is off, but you can't quite figure out what?

Are you wondering how you went from being adored, idolized and worshipped to devalued, demeaned and discarded? Are you banging your head against the wall trying to figure out how your relationship went from a fairy-tale to a train-wreck over night?

Stop!!!!!

You have done nothing wrong. You may be in a relationship with a narcissist.

It is very difficult to see what lies underneath the charisma of a narcissist. A narcissist is like a wolf in sheep's clothing...charming, alluring, and often the life of the party. The beginning of the relationship is euphoric, intense and exhilarating. It is like nothing you have ever experienced before, and you can't get enough of your newfound love.

You are put on a pedestal and told all your little quirks are endearing and adorable. You have never felt so incredibly loved by another person in all your life. A narcissist sweeps you off your feet and appears more caring and compassionate than any person you have ever met. Unfortunately, once you settle down with a narcissist, you will see a side of him you never knew existed. A side, quite frankly, you would rather not acknowledge.

Underneath the flashy exterior of a narcissist is a fragile ego, which requires constant attention and validation. The implications this has on a relationship are far more damaging than you could ever imagine. Eventually, a narcissist will discard, devalue, belittle and criticize you. Emotional abuse is inevitable in any long-term relationship with a narcissist. The abuse is not only devastating, but comes out of nowhere and causes you to question everything you thought you ever knew.

It is important to understand that narcissists are incapable of reciprocating love, which makes healthy relationships with them impossible. In the beginning, they seem to be overly compassionate and caring, but eventually you realize, they have simply put on an act in order to win and secure your love. The only reason a narcissist seeks out a relationship is to ensure someone is always present to meet his never-ending needs.

My ex-husband was a narcissist. Not just someone who exhibited narcissistic tendencies, but someone who was diagnosed with pathological narcissism by his own therapist.

Someone's narcissism is labeled pathological when it becomes so extreme they have no ability to recognize other people as independent of themselves. They literally believe the world revolves around them and people exist to accomodate their needs. It is not just selfish, arrogant behavior that makes a relationship with someone like this difficult. It is much more complicated and thus, important to understand and recognize as early as possible.

My ex-husband joked from day one about being a narcissist. Unfortunately, it took me eight years to look into the true meaning of narcissism and how it impacts a relationship. When I did, it explained everything to me and opened up a whole new world for me. I have made it a goal to share what I have learned with others so they don't live in the dark like I did for years.

Knowledge is power and can be truly liberating.

I wrote my first book, *It's All About Him,* to build awareness and help others recognize a narcissist before getting involved. I also started an on-line support forum at **www.ThePathForwardNow.com** where members talk about their attempt to love a narcissist. No one knows what it is like to be in a relationship with a narcissist unless they have been through it themselves. Being able to talk to others who are going through a similar experience is very cathartic. Our forum is a safe haven for members to share their story with others who can relate on a level no on else can.

Research tells us narcissism is on the rise. [1] As a result, more and more of us are finding ourselves in relationships with people who do not know how to relate to us. It is important to understand if you're involved with a narcissist, he will never change and is incapable of changing. You either accept him for who he is or you move on.

A relationship with a narcissist is toxic. A toxic relationship is one in which you do all the giving and the other person does nothing but take. It is a relationship where you shower your partner with love and affection only to receive little to no love or affection in return. It is a relationship that begins like a dream, but quickly turns into an emotional roller-coaster ride you can't get off no matter how hard you try. It is critical you understand why relationships with narcissists do not work and realize it is not your fault. It is the pathology of the personality disorder that prevents true reciprocity of love and fuels the abuse.

I am frequently asked how to get over a narcissist. While there is no magic pill, you CAN and you WILL survive. Our current forum is full of great ideas and suggestions from members getting over these emotionally abusive partnerships. Based on the collective wisdom of this amazing group, dedicated forum moderators, personal experience and lots of research, I have developed 6 Steps I believe will help you recover and move forward.

It is my sincere hope and belief that the following steps will help you understand what you experienced, process your pain, and heal. Nothing here is rocket science and some of it may even feel like common sense. However, it is important to me to provide my readers with a path to recovery. Based on my personal journey, this is what has worked for me.

The Path FORWARD!

Step 1 – Understand It

We educate ourselves on the personality of a narcissist.

Step 2 – Get It Out

We find an outlet to share and express our emotions.

Step 3 – No Contact

We accept the only way to restore our sanity and regain control of our lives is through *No Contact*.

Step 4 – Get Real

We no longer deny reality and are ready to face our anger and fear.

Step 5 – Wake Up

We tap into the power of our mind to awaken our spirit and find ourselves again.

Step 6 – Heal

We have a newfound compassion for ourselves and commit to live in the moment.

Once we learn to see the narcissist for the person he really is, we are finally able to free ourselves. We realize we do not need this person in our lives to feel whole and complete. We were whole and complete before this person entered our lives and we will be whole and complete once we end our relationship with this person. It is the narcissist who is preventing us from being truly happy. It is so important you understand this.   .

NOTHING stands between you and your true self, but the narcissist in your life!

CHAPTER 1

STEP ONE
UNDERSTAND IT

We educate ourselves on the personality of a narcissist.

Being in a relationship with a narcissist is like being on a roller-coaster ride that never ends. One moment, you feel loved, adored and cherished. The next, you feel devalued, discarded and abused. Narcissists have often been described as having a Dr. Jekyll and Mr. Hyde personality. They engage in "crazy-making" behavior to make you feel as though you are losing your mind.

You never know what kind of mood a narcissist is going to be in and you certainly never know how he is going to treat you. A narcissist is unpredictable and unstable. You are always walking on eggshells around him. He wants to keep you guessing and doubting yourself at all times.

We all possess narcissistic tendencies. It is important to understand that narcissism falls on a spectrum. When a person's narcissism becomes so severe that it consumes them, it develops into a pathological personality disorder called Narcissistic Personality Disorder.

Put simply, pathological behavior describes anything carried to such an extreme that it becomes abnormal. A narcissist is so wrapped-up in himself that he cannot feel emotions for others. He is incapable of reciprocating love or feeling empathy for anyone. He does not experience these feelings as we do. As a result, doing things for others is pointless to him. His entire life revolves around doing things to please himself.

A narcissist has delusions of grandeur that are so severe, it is impossible to live with him and maintain any modicum of sanity. The sense of entitlement a narcissist feels is mind-boggling, to say the least. A narcissist is always right and believes others should feel honored to be in the presence of his greatness.

Charlie Sheen's comments in his infamous war with Warner Brothers provide the perfect example of such "crazy-making" behavior.

- "I am on a drug. It's called Charlie Sheen. It's not available. If you try it once, you will die. Your face will melt off and your children will weep over your exploded body."

- "I got magic and I've got poetry in my fingertips, you know, most of the time, and this includes naps. I'm an F-18, bro."

- "If you're a part of my family, I will love you violently."

- "AA was written for normal people. People that don't have tiger blood and Adonis DNA. . . I have a different brain, I have a different heart. I got tiger blood, man."

- "I'm tired of pretending like I'm not special. I'm tired of pretending like I'm not bitchin', a total freakin' rock star from Mars."

- "We work for the pope, we murder people. We're Vatican assassins. How complicated can it be? What they're not ready for is guys like you and I and Nails and all the other gnarly gnarlingtons in my life, that we are high priests, Vatican assassin warlocks. Boom. Print that, people."

- "I closed my eyes and in a nanosecond I cured myself."

- "The last time I took drugs, I probably took more than anyone could survive. I was banging 7-gram rocks because that's how I roll, I have one speed, go.

- "What's not to love? Especially when you see how I party, it was epic. The run I was on made Sinatra, Flynn, Jagger, Richards and all of them look like droopy-eyed armless children."

- "Winning!"

Clearly, this is delusional behavior indicative of someone who suffers from Narcissistic Personality Disorder. Unfortunately, just like Mr. Sheen, narcissists are great actors, which serves them very well in the beginning of a relationship. A narcissist is like a chameleon. He will figure out what you're looking for in a man and then mold himself into this image in order to win you over.

Once a narcissist has your heart, his true colors emerge and the reality of his true persona is quite shocking. Once in control, a narcissist becomes demeaning and cruel. He will devalue and discard you within time. It is inevitable in any long-term relationship with a narcissist.

It is critical to our recovery that we understand why the narcissist behaves the way he does. More importantly, we must understand that we have done NOTHING to bring about this drastic change in his behavior. We must accept there is absolutely NOTHING we can do to bring back the man we fell in love with and adore. We suddenly realize this man never existed. He simply put on an act to win us over.

Accepting this is not easy, but it is imperative we understand this in order to move on. We need to get real with ourselves about what happened in our relationship. Only by understanding the narcissist do we realize we have suffered emotional abuse and trauma at the hands of the person we love.

Knowledge is Power!

Before we continue, please allow me to clarify that both men and women suffer from Narcissistic Personality Disorder (NPD). Men typically have more opportunities to be in a position where they can abuse their power. Studies tell us 75% of narcissists are male. However, it is important to note that a woman can be just as narcissistic as a man.

I will refer to the narcissist as a male for purposes of flow and brevity. It is simply easier to read if I'm not constantly referring to both sexes. Therefore, if you are involved in a relationship with a female narcissist, please replace the male pronoun with the female pronoun.

Narcissists can emulate emotions better than anyone. While they initially appear more sympathetic than the average person, the truth is, they are incapable of feeling emotions. Of course you're probably thinking to yourself, everyone has feelings. You may think that feelings are instinctual and we are all born with the ability to feel. You're right. All humans have emotions. However, everyone is different in how they relate to their feelings.

I am not a mental health professional, but I have learned one basic and fundamental truth about humans and their emotions: Some individuals are more in touch with their feelings than others. Humans have found many ways of numbing themselves in an effort to avoid having to feel. For some, drinking alcohol or doing drugs helps numb unwanted feelings and allows an individual to disconnect from himself for a short while.

Some individuals eventually learn not only how to numb their pain, but develop an ability to disconnect from themselves and their feelings altogether. They separate from their emotions because they have learned their feelings do not help them. They only cause them pain. This describes the emotional state of a narcissist.

One of the most well-known theories in psychology is Sigmund Freud's theory that as children, we pass through different psychosexual stages. According to Freud, if a child is over-indulged or under-indulged in any of these stages, it results in what he calls fixation. Fixation describes an adult who is stuck or attached to an earlier childhood mode of satisfaction.

An infant does not see others as indistinguishable from the self. An infant or small child perceives the world as an extension of himself.

Children feel that people, particularly mother, are present to cater to their every need. They know that if they cry, they can elicit an immediate response in those around them. They will be presented with food and cradling in response to any fussing or crying on their part. They see others as existing solely for their purpose.

This type of selfishness is natural for an infant or small child. They must rely on others to meet their needs in order to survive. According to Freud, this extreme selfishness, or narcissism, is a normal psychosexual stage of development between the stages of auto-eroticism and object-libido.

Children eventually grow out of this narcissistic stage. They grow out of it and learn to understand that others have needs as well. Unfortunately, not everyone grows out of this stage. If they received too much or too little attention, they become fixated in this stage, obsessed with getting their needs met at all times.

Sadly, a narcissist was either neglected as a child or over-indulged. He is stuck. He never developed the more complex feelings that make us uniquely human, like love and empathy. He does not relate to the world or others in the same way we do. A narcissist is emotionally stunted and disconnected from his true self. The easiest way to think of him is as a five or six year old child who has yet to understand that he is not the center of everyone's universe.

Since narcissists are not in touch with their true self, they are dependent on others to fill a void. Unfortunately, no one can ever fill this void because their expectations are unrealistic, unattainable and ever-changing. No one will ever be good enough for them and they will repeat this cycle of abusing and discarding romantic partners throughout their lives.

There is much confusion and pain when in a relationship with a narcissist. We repeatedly find ourselves let down and disappointed by our partner. We have given our heart and soul to this person, but they cannot return our love and we do not understand why. Often, we deny the reality of our situation for years before we get honest with ourselves.

Getting over a relationship with a narcissist is not the same as with a healthy well-adjusted adult. In a typical breakup, we grieve the loss of love, the pain of saying goodbye, the sadness of something wonderful ending, broken promises and halted dreams.

When grieving a narcissist, this pain is compounded by the reality that this person is not who you thought he was at all. Thinking you know someone and then suddenly being confronted with a person you don't even recognize is quite a shock to the system. He professed his undying love for you one moment, but then abandoned you the next by either emotionally withdrawing or physically leaving. You realize he never loved you and simply used you to meet his never-ending child-like needs.

"The eye sees only what the mind is prepared to comprehend."
~ Henri L. Bergson

What is narcissistic personality disorder?

Certainly, only a certified mental health professional can diagnose someone with pathological narcissism. For your reference, below is the definition the American Psychological Association (APA) has published in its current version of the Diagnostic & Statistics Manual.

Narcissistic Personality Disorder **(DSM-IV code 301.81)**

According to the APA, a person suffers from Narcissistic Personality Disorder (NPD) if they exhibit five or more of the following characteristics:

1) Has a grandiose sense of self-importance (e.g., exaggerates achievements and talents, expects to be recognized as superior without commensurate achievements)

2) Is preoccupied with fantasies of unlimited success, power, brilliance, beauty, or ideal love

3) Believes that he or she is "special" and unique and can only be understood by, or should associate with, other special or high-status people (or institutions)

4) Requires excessive admiration

5) Has a sense of entitlement, i.e., unreasonable expectations of especially favorable treatment or automatic compliance with his or her expectations

6) Is interpersonally exploitative, i.e., takes advantage of others to achieve his or her own ends

7) Lacks empathy: is unwilling to recognize or identify with the feelings and needs of others

8) Is often envious of others or believes that others are envious of him or her

9) Shows arrogant, haughty behaviors or attitudes

Why do they devalue & discard us?

Unfortunately, once a narcissist is victorious and secures your love, the idealization phase of the relationship passes and his true colors emerge. You begin to see the pathology of his personality and realize he merely put on an act in the beginning of the relationship to win and secure your love. He becomes demanding and angry, unaware that you have needs or a separate self at all. He simply finds it impossible to see you as an independent entity.

"Women know intuitively when they are being devalued."
~ Robyn Silverman

Trying to understand how you went from being idolized and put on a pedestal to being completely discarded is baffling. Suddenly, you can't do anything right and nothing you do is good enough for him. By understanding the inevitable Devalue & Discard (D&D) behavior of a narcissist, you will finally realize what happened and know that you did NOTHING wrong to cause such a drastic change in his behavior.

It is important to understand when in a toxic relationship, you are viewed as nothing more than an extension of your narcissist. Narcissists seek out relationships in order to ensure someone is present to cater to their needs, stroke their ego and make them look good. Men often select a trophy wife. Beautiful women are the ultimate status symbol for men….proof of their masculinity and virility. On the other hand, female narcissists are typically attracted to wealthy men who can support their obsession with image and status.

A narcissist will eventually devalue and discard you with no remorse. It is inevitable in any relationship with a narcissist. At some point, he will emotionally and physically withdraw from you and leave you wondering what you did wrong. Please remember, you did NOTHING wrong. It has NOTHING to do with you. A narcissist is unable to attach in a healthy way to anyone. Ultimately, he will pull away no matter what you do.

A narcissist has a lot of built-up resentment toward his significant other. He knows he is reliant on you for validation. However, he craves variety and is easily bored. As a result, he blames you for tying him down to a monotonous and mundane lifestyle. This creates in him a great deal of anger towards you because he does not want to rely on you, yet knows he must in order to get the validation he so desperately needs. He does not respect you because he knows you put up with a lot of abuse from him. You have done nothing wrong but be overly giving and nurturing. Yet he is angry with you and blames you for all of his unhappiness.

He is urgent, preoccupied with himself and always trying to right his chronic imbalance. While some narcissists do not feel the emptiness in their lives, their behavior causes major suffering and angst among those around them. Once a narcissist feels he has obtained control of you, you will see a completely different side of him you never knew existed. Once in control, a narcissist becomes demeaning and cruel.

Narcissists are oblivious to others and how their behavior affects people close to them. They dismiss the feelings, ideas, and opinions of others. They are condescending in their nature. They belittle, criticize, judge and put others down.

A narcissist can be blatant about it or quite subtle in his approach. He has a way of putting you down in such a way that you don't even realize you have been insulted until you reflect upon the conversation later or someone points it out to you. Other times, he can be brutally offensive. They have no shame.

While narcissists do not always realize how hurtful their behavior is, it doesn't mean at times, they are not deliberately abusive. A narcissist is purposefully abusive when his relationship with you changes in a way that is not to his liking. This occurs whenever he starts to feel too close to you. Intimacy terrifies a narcissist, and he will respond by being abusive in order to push you away.

Another example of when a narcissist is intentionally abusive is if you voice your displeasure or threaten to leave the relationship. A narcissist cannot be alone. He is terrified of being alone and must always have someone present to validate him. By asserting abusive behavior, he is attempting to maintain his dominance and control over you.

A narcissist has a way of turning everything around so you begin to question yourself. He will do something terribly mean or cruel. You will talk to him about it, and by the end of the conversation, you are the one apologizing for some reason. A narcissist knows how to manipulate better than anyone.

A narcissist eventually becomes sarcastic and belittles you constantly. You begin to feel you can do nothing right in his eyes and your presence is hardly tolerable. You're baffled. You wonder what you did wrong to cause such a drastic change in his feelings toward you. You struggle desperately to return things to the way they were in the beginning. Unfortunately, as hard as you try, things will never be the same again. He is not the man you thought he was. It is a maddening and precarious way to live and can drive anyone to the edge of their sanity.

When a narcissist feels he is in control of you and is not threatened by any fear that you will ask for too much from him or leave the relationship, he will engage in escapist activity and appear as if he hardly knows you exist the majority of the time. You are merely present to validate him should he not get enough attention from the outside world that day.

You are treated with indifference by the person who once showered you with love and affection. His "silent treatment" is his way of devaluing you. If you begin to pull away, he will lay on the charm again. A narcissist knows when to engage his false self to ensure you never leave him. He is always reminding you that he understands you like no one else can or ever will. It is essential that he makes you believe only he can understand you. By constantly telling you that you have problems and quirks only he can understand, he believes you will become dependent on him. By telling you he loves you despite your flaws, he hopes you will begin to feel unlovable in some strange paranoid way.

17

This is his way of ensuring you will never leave him. It is narcissistic manipulation at its finest and it is important that you recognize it.

A narcissist will always ensure he has someone present and available to him at all times to validate him. Unfortunately, he will give you no warning when he decides to leave in pursuit of validation from someone new. This is when we must remember we did NOTHING wrong and this outcome was inevitable.

A narcissist will simply discard you when he becomes convinced that you can no longer provide him with sufficient validation. Keep in mind, this evaluation of his is totally subjective and not grounded in reality at all. Suddenly, because of boredom, a disagreement, an act or a failure to act, he swings from total idolization to complete devaluation.

He then disconnects from you immediately. He needs to preserve all of his energy in order to obtain and secure new sources of supply. He sees no need to spend any of his precious time and energy on you, whom he now considers useless.

You must accept the fact that you were not an object of love to this person, but a pawn, a mere source of supply to feed his fragile ego; nothing more, but certainly nothing less.

Once you understand how he must constantly change his source of supply, you will realize his rejection of you has NOTHING to do with you. He will repeat this cycle in every relationship he enters. It is inevitable. Be grateful this toxic abusive man is out of your life and never let him back.

Why can't they change?

People with Narcissistic Personality Disorder are rigid and often unaware that their thoughts and behavior patterns are inappropriate. Research indicates they are rarely the ones who come in for treatment. Instead, the spouse, significant other, children, and parents of the personality disordered are the ones who suffer and seek therapy. Narcissists do not typically seek treatment.

Furthermore, personality disorders begin in adolescence/early adulthood and do not change over time. While narcissists often have a hard time dealing with stress and may have symptoms such as substance abuse or anxiety that can be treated with medication, it is important to understand that the personality disorder itself cannot be treated. These personality traits are so deeply ingrained that they defy change.

One analogy that illustrates the permanence of a personality disorder is to compare it to a mental illness. Mental illnesses (such as Schizophrenia or Bipolar Disorder) can be treated with medication and cognitive therapy. Most mental illnesses are caused by disruptions in brain cell receptors and synapses, which are believed to be genetically inherited. As long as someone with Schizophrenia or Bipolar disorder is committed to taking their medication regularly, symptoms subside and they feel and act relatively normal.

The onset of mental illness is typically quite sudden and profound. It is often described as though a heavy wool blanket has descended upon a person's personality and smothered it. A personality disorder, on the other hand, is all pervasive.

With mental illness, a person's personality is smothered or blanketed by the onset of the illness. Medication used to restore proper chemical balance in the brain helps to remove the blanket and bring back the true personality of the individual.

In contrast, the personality of someone with a personality disorder is virtually interwoven into every fiber of that blanket. It is the fabric and foundation of who they are. If you unravel the blanket, you unravel the person's entire personality.

Therefore, the way I see it is simple: you have two choices. You either accept your partner for who he is or you move on. It is critical that you understand you have done NOTHING wrong nor is there anything you can do to change the situation. It is not your fault. You fell in love with someone who is incapable of having an adult mature relationship.

Personality disorders cannot be treated. Sometimes in life we must accept the fact that the only person we can change is ourselves. I know I have learned this lesson more than once in my life. It is not an easy lesson, but it is an important one. Accepting that there is nothing you can do to improve your relationship with the person you love is painful, but powerful.

Why must we get real to heal?

The painful part is obvious. Loving someone who cannot return your love is agonizing and difficult to accept. However, the knowledge that no matter what you do, this person will never change is quite powerful, in my opinion. Once you understand this fundamental truth, a whole new world opens up to you. Your newfound knowledge should be liberating.

When in a relationship with a narcissist, we often lie to ourselves in order to keep going. We lie to ourselves that things aren't as bad as they really are. We do not want to accept that the person we fell in love with is not who we thought he was in the beginning. No one wants to admit this. Why would we want to admit this without a fight? We have invested so much in this relationship. We do not want to believe that our soul mate is not real. We would rather exhaust every possibile excuse or explanation we can before we admit this inconvenient truth to ourselves.

I lied to myself for years about my ex-husband, refusing to see the side of him I didn't want to see. Unfortunately, lying to yourself like this forces you to disconnect from your true self just like the narcissist did as a child. Trust me, this is no way to live. Denial is akin to death. When you disconnect from yourself, I believe you die a slow death inside. You become your own worst enemy. Subconsciously, you know you're lying to yourself. You know you are denying your reality, burying your head in the sand and living in the dark.

No matter how hard we try to fool the mind into thinking everything is ok, it knows the truth. The mind is amazingly powerful. We may try to avoid thinking about it by keeping ourselves busy with work or projects. We may even try to numb ourselves with alcohol, but at the end of the day, we know we are lying to ourselves.

In order to keep the lie alive, you disconnect from yourself. You then begin to get angry with yourself for not being strong enough to face reality. Anger turned inward turns into depression. So now, not only are you miserable in your relationship, but you feel dead inside, angry and depressed.

"When one is pretending, the entire body revolts." ~ Anais Nin

We cannot avoid reality. We have to be honest with ourselves. If not, we lose all trust in ourselves. We must *Get Real to Heal*, as I like to say. When I finally got real and faced reality, it explained everything to me and gave me a second chance at life and love. We will talk in more detail about the importance of getting real in a later chapter.

For now, it is important to understand that the only closure you can possibly hope for in a relationship with a narcissist is the knowledge that this person is permanently disordered and disturbed. He will never change. You must accept him for who he is and all his limitations or move on and create a new life for yourself.

I believe in creating a new life. We owe it to ourselves. There is no question that we deserve real and authentic love. Life is short. There are people out there capable of genuine love and we deserve nothing less. In order to receive it, we must first be honest with ourselves about the reality of our situation and face the truth. This way we can make ourselves available when the real deal comes along.

Why do they seek out relationships?

So you're probably asking yourself why someone so self-absorbed would have any interest in pursuing a relationship with someone else. What you have to understand is that a narcissist is looking for meaning to fill up his emptiness. A narcissist has no inner sense of self and requires someone prove to him that he exists by reflecting his image back to him.

Narcissists need people more than anyone. They have very specific reasons for being in relationships, but they are not built on the universal need we all have, which is to love. They do not enter or stay in relationships for love. Their motives are quite different. They become involved in relationships in order to ensure their needs are met and someone is always present to provide them with the attention and adoration they require in order to feel alive.

Narcissists feed off of attention. Adoration from others is what fuels them. It is like a drug to them and they are addicted to it. Sam Vaknin, a self-professed narcissist and author of "Malignant Self-Love — Narcissism Revisited" calls this drug Narcissistic Supply (NS). NS is any form of attention an individual receives from others.[1]

According to Vaknin, there are two types of Narcissistic Supply—Primary and Secondary. Primary Narcissistic Supply is the day-to-day changing attention a narcissist receives from various different people he encounters throughout his day. When a narcissist does not receive enough Primary NS from strangers or others to fulfill his desires, he resorts to what is called Secondary NS.

Secondary Narcissistic Supply is strictly for backup purposes. Secondary NS is obtained from a narcissist's significant other. The significant other is a constant presence in the narcissist's life. Therefore, they are always available and accessible to him, should he encounter deficient Primary NS at some point during the day.

A narcissist needs to ensure he has a constant and reliable source of supply at all times. The best way he has found of doing this is to have a significant other in his life. He does not love this person, nor does he wish to be with this person most of the time. However, because it is impossible to control how much attention or Primary NS he will receive from the outside world on a daily basis, he must make certain he has a backup form of it that is always available to him. It is for this reason a narcissist seeks to find a significant other. He prefers Primary NS because it is ever-changing and dynamic, but when unavailable, he will resort to Secondary NS ... a.k.a. his significant other.

"Never allow someone to be your priority while allowing yourself to be their option." ~ Mark Twain

What is the ego-self?

The following terms have been used interchangeably in our culture for years: real self, true self, inner child, higher self. These terms refer to the same core part in humans. It is who we are when we feel most authentic or genuine. Our true self is loving, giving, expressive, creative, and spontaneous. Overall, we feel whole and alive when we are in touch with our true self. This feeling of wholeness and happiness can only come to us when we are open, honest and real with ourselves. We refer to this as the Real-Self.

In contrast, what has been called the false self, unauthentic self, or public self describes how we feel when we are uncomfortable or strained. Alienated from the true self, our false self is egocentric, selfish, withholding, envious, and critical. This is what we call the Ego-Self. The Ego-Self is attached to material things and physical image. The Ego-Self prohibits us from being in touch with our true inner self, which is required in order to attain any level of spirituality, in my opinion.

The Ego-Self is often used by individuals as a way to cover up their true feelings. The Ego-Self is inhibited and fearful. Once formed and functioning, the Ego-Self stifles the growth of the Real-Self. The more developed one's Ego-Self becomes, the more nonexistent the Real-Self becomes.

Healthy well-adjusted people engage their Real-Self the majority of the time. The Ego-Self is reserved only for situations in which one feels threatened or uneasy. The Ego-Self is often used as a defense mechanism. The Ego-Self often feels the need to impress others.

All of us are guilty of engaging the Ego-Self from time to time. It typically happens when we're in a stressful situation, nervous or distracted. We just can't seem to be ourselves. We may find ourselves saying something silly to impress someone else without even realizing how ridiculous we sound. It can happen to anyone depending on what is going on in their lives at the time. If we are distracted and not able to focus on the moment, we may try to fill space by saying something without thinking. Bottom line is when we engage our Ego-Self, we are NOT being authentic.

The Real-Self has more compassion for others and encourages an authentic interaction where we can truly be ourselves. We are comfortable being ourselves and can drop all defenses. The Ego-Self, on the other hand, refuses to look at reality or face difficult issues.

It is important to understand that the Real-Self plays NO role (active or passive) in the conscious life of a narcissist. That is because a narcissist's Ego-Self has completely killed off his Real-Self. A narcissist is dead inside and will always rely on others to validate his existence.

The Ego-Self serves many functions to a narcissist, the most important being that it acts as a shield or barrier to anyone who could potentially hurt, upset, or disappoint him. The Ego-Self can absorb any amount of pain. The Ego-Self feels the need to dominate and control, seeing others as nothing more than pawns in a quest for power.

A narcissist typically invents his Ego-Self as a child. By inventing it, he develops immunity to any abuse, indifference, smothering, or exploitation he may fall victim to as a child. He does not want to feel the feelings this mistreatment causes. Therefore, he invents an Ego-Self to protect himself from the pain.

By projecting an Ego-Self to others, a narcissist is able to live in a fantasy world of his own creation. His Ego-Self acts as a defense shield to ensure his Real-Self (buried deep within) can never be hurt again. It essentially protects him from the pain of his reality. Unfortunately, it also kills his spirit, disconnects him, deadens him inside and prohibits him from attaching to any other human in a healthy way.

Why can't it ever work?

As you now know, narcissists disconnect from themselves as children. What may be even more important for you to understand, however, is not only has a narcissist disconnected from himself, but he will NEVER allow himself to connect with another person under any circumstance.

A narcissist lives in a world of fear. He is afraid of being exposed, afraid of being abandoned and afraid of losing control. Living in a state of fear like this causes him to always be in a fight or flight mode. He is always on the defense and unable to let his guard down. As a result, he does not attach to others in a healthy way and inevitably destroys any trust that once existed in a relationship. The demise of a healthy relationship with a narcissist is unavoidable.

Why can't they love?

Narcissists are incapable of feeling love or empathy. It is critical that you understand this. They are stunted emotionally and never developed the feelings that make us uniquely human, such as compassion and love.

Healthy, well-adjusted children eventually grow out of the narcissistic stage. They grow out of it and learn to understand that others have needs as well. Unfortunately, not everyone grows out of this stage. If they were neglected or over-indulged as a child, they become fixated in this stage, obsessed with getting their needs met at all times. This is where the narcissist is stuck. He is stuck at age five and completely oblivious to the fact that others have needs or wants of their own.

The only feelings a narcissist experiences are the primal, instinctive gut feelings we all possess in order to survive – Anger and Fear. We are all born with these instincts as they are critical to our survival (i.e. Darwin's Theory).

This also helps explain why when a narcissist becomes upset, he is capable of fierce rage, right? That's because anger and fear are the only real feelings a narcissist experiences. Therefore, when he feels these feelings, watch out. This is no acting. This is true and authentic rage.

It is actually quite sad. Narcissists are not able to experience the range of emotions we can. They will never encounter pure joy, compassion or true love. Sure, they think they love you but that's because they are dependent on you for survival, not because they are in love with you in any mature, adult or romantic way.

Let me be clear, you did mean something to the narcissist. You made

him feel alive. A narcissist only spends time with people who inspire and excite him. However, at the end of the day, a narcissist is incapable of feeling genuine love and will inevitably move on in pursuit of new supply. His attention is always fleeting and only temporary. He is always looking for the next best high, like a drug addict.

Unfortunately, he cannot help it. Narcissists never develop the complex, evolved feelings that make us human. Deep down they know they are different. They know they should feel these feelings and learn to mimic this behavior by watching others. They do not want to be "found out" so they "act out" the feelings they know they should feel in the beginning of a relationship in order to win your love. Unfortunately, this is only an act and once they feel confident that they have secured your love, their true colors will emerge.

Why can't they accept love?

Narcissists might hope for love and caring, but feel very uncomfortable if they seem to find it. Being in love makes them feel vulnerable and this terrifies them. They doubt the authenticity of real love and devalue anyone who loves them because they believe that person, like themselves, can never live up to their expectations of perfection.

Narcissists cannot grasp the concept of unconditional love that includes the acceptance of flaws. Love does not sustain them. Instead it feels unsafe. Admiration feels safer because it can be earned through achievements and credentials. Since these are things they can control, they feel much safer being admired, rather than loved.

As a result, they seek attention and admiration from as many people as possible. Those who profess their love are eventually discarded and devalued. Narcissists are unaware of how they vacillate between idolizing and devaluing their significant other. At the end of the day, however, it is important to understand:

A narcissist would rather be admired by many than loved by one.

Why do they dread intimacy?

Narcissists dread intimacy and view it as weak. In their mind, becoming intimate with someone cancels their superiority and demystifies them. They thrive on being unique and in control.

To illustrate this, I will use Sam Vaknin's description of the two types of narcissists: Cerebral Narcissist or Somatic Narcissist. Vaknin believes when narcissists create and project a false image of who they wish to be, they are either Cerebral (intellectual) or Somatic (sexual). In other words, they either attract attention by applying their intellect/talent or by applying their sexuality/bodies. [2]

Narcissists know by perfecting their looks or exhibiting superior intellect or talent, they will obtain the adoration they so badly crave. Female narcissists are known for using their *physical assets* to lure their victims and men often use their *position of power*. Once they determine what they possess that best attracts attention, they will perfect it and hone it like nothing else. They are addicted to attention and will create and project an Ego-Self they are certain will attract the most attention.

The *Somatic Narcissist* flaunts his body, exhibits his muscles, and brags about his sexual conquests. An example of this type of narcissist would be a professional athlete, model, or stripper. A *Cerebral Narcissist* is an elitist. He uses his intellect, knowledge, or talent to attract attention. An example of this type of narcissist would be a politician, writer or professor. All narcissists are both cerebral and somatic. However, one type is always dominant in a narcissist. The narcissist may swing between his dominant type and recessive type, but he prefers utilizing one over the other.

Cerebral (intellectual) Narcissists regard sex as a chore ... something they must do in order to maintain their source of Narcissistic Supply ... a.k.a. their significant other. *Somatic (sexual) Narcissists* derive validation from their sexual conquests. In the dating world, the trend of "hooking up" or sleeping around is perfect for narcissists of this type. They love to brag to others about their physical conquests and view sexual partners as nothing more than sex objects who allow them to obtain Narcissistic Supply.

Narcissists have intimacy issues and cannot see their partner in a healthy way. They are unable to see what most people dream of in a lover—someone who is both sweet and sexy at the same time. They cannot help categorizing people into one of two separate categories—saintly or sexy. They find it impossible to see someone as both. To them, someone is one or the other, but never both. This is what psychologists refer to as a *Madonna-Whore Complex.*

For example, in a heterosexual relationship, if a woman is sweet and nice, the narcissist classifies her as a Madonna. If she treats him badly, she is defined as a Whore. A Madonna is sexless. A Whore turns a Narcissist on like nothing else. In the beginning of a relationship, every woman is sexy to a narcissist because the thrill of the chase makes her enticing. The harder to get she plays, the sexier she becomes. However, once she has been conquered by the narcissist, she slowly loses her desirability. The more comfortable the relationship becomes and the more caring she becomes, the less enticing she is to him sexually. She loses her sex appeal and becomes a saintly Madonna figure.

A Madonna fulfills a narcissist's need to be catered to like a child. A Whore fulfills his adult sexual needs. A Whore is the type of woman that turns a narcissist on. A Madonna is completely sexless. Over time, any woman who is good and caring to a narcissist will inevitably become sexless.

This is when a *Somatic Narcissist* will begin having sexual encounters outside the relationship and feel as though he is entitled to cheat on you. *Cerebral Narcissists* are more likely to revert to pornography at this point. Many become addicted to pornography because they are auto-erotic and prefer to masturbate than be intimate with another person.

In an interview for Playboy, John Mayer said he would rather masturbate by himself than be with a real woman. In my opinion, this man is a perfect example of a raging narcissist who has significant *Madonna-Whore* issues.

I believe the easy and instant access teenagers have to pornography today contributes to the development of a *Madonna-Whore Complex*. When a teenager is repeatedly exposed to pornography, it can skew their understanding of intimacy. Instead of learning that sex is something you save for someone you love, they see people having sex with many random people in pornography.

What does this teach teens about sex? It tells them that sex is not sacred. It teaches them that sex need not be reserved for only the one you love. Many teens today are learning about sex and love through pornography. As a result, they see the two as mutually exclusive. Just like the narcissist, they believe love is sexless, pure, and saintly; whereas sex is dirty and reserved for Whores. I believe this is one example of how modern society contributes to the increase of narcissism in our society.

Whether they revert to pornography or begin sleeping with others, the narcissist will always perceive the object of his sexual desire as dirty because that is the only thing that turns him on. A woman who is kind, sweet, and giving will always be viewed as a saintly, sexless Madonna to the narcissist. Those who act like Whores turn him on like nothing else.

A narcissist eventually withdraws sexually from any type of intimate relationship you once had with him. It is inevitable in any long-term relationship with a narcissist. You become sexless. He still needs you, no doubt. However, this is only because he needs you to cater to his child-like needs. He needs you to ensure that someone will always be present to validate him, should the outside world fall short of his expectations.

How do they brainwash us?

Narcissists lead us to believe we have something we actually do not have, and we hold on to it. We think we have a relationship with an amazing person, when in reality we are living with an illusion that our relationship is special. The acting talent these personalities possess is astounding. They are brilliant con-artists and we must accept that the wonderful person we fell in love with NEVER existed. He hid behind a mask of smoke and mirrors in order to obtain control of us and manipulate us to meet his never-ending child-like needs. Once we learn to see the narcissist for the person he really is, we are finally able to free ourselves.

The emotional abuse that occurs in a relationship with a narcissist is merciless and relentless. Narcissists brainwash us. They use several different methods of coercion in order to obtain control over us. They threaten, degrade, shift blame, criticize, manipulate, verbally assault, dominate, blackmail, withdraw, withhold love and affection and gaslight us.

The dictionary definition of *gaslighting* is "to drive someone crazy" and narcissists use this method to keep their victims under their control. The term *gaslighting* was coined in the movie "Gaslight" from the 1940s. Ingrid Bergman won an Oscar for her portrayal of a wife who is made to believe by her husband that she is going crazy and imagining things so he can gain access to her inheritance. He repeatedly lights a gas lamp

in one part of the house, causing the other lamps to become dimmer. When Bergman's character asks her husband about this, he denies that it's happening and tells her she is seeing things.

Put quite simply, *gaslighting* is a form of brainwashing. The narcissist denies that events ever occurred or certain things were said. This causes the victim to doubt what they're hearing and seeing to the point that they begin to question their sanity. A member of *The Path Forward Now* Forum was married to a man who would sneak into her closet to tighten the waist line of her pants and skirts to make her believe she was gaining weight!

Over time, the victim begins to believe the gaslighter and essentially succumbs to their brainwashing. They start to think they are imagining things and have some kind of mental illness or faulty memory. When one doubts their perception of reality, the gaslighter is able to control that person because they become completely dependent on the gaslighter for the truth.

A common tactic of a narcissist is to project their own issues on to their victim. *Projection* should be their middle name. They do this in an attempt to hide any actions or truths they do not want brought to light about themselves. It is their hope that by projecting issues of their own onto you it will distract you from noticing their malignant behavior.

A narcissist wants you to believe you have problems and issues only he can understand and only he is willing to tolerate. By doing this, he believes you will begin to feel unlovable and never leave him out of fear of rejection in the future.

Sam Vaknin does an excellent job of describing how a narcissist abuses his victim when he writes:

"He infiltrates her defenses, shatters her self-confidence, confuses and confounds her, demeans and debases her. He invades her territory, abuses her confidence, exhausts her resources, hurts her loved ones, threatens her stability and security, involves her in his paranoid states of mind, frightens her out of her wits, withholds love and sex from her, prevents satisfaction and causes frustration, humiliates and insults her privately and in public, points out her shortcomings, criticizes her profusely and in a "scientific and objective" manner – and this is a partial list. Very often, the narcissist acts sadistically in the guise of an enlightened interest in the welfare of his victim. He plays the psychiatrist to her psychopathology (totally dreamt up by him). He acts the guru to her need of guidance, the avuncular or father figure, the teacher, the only true friend, the old and the experienced. All this in order to weaken her defenses and to lay siege to her disintegrating nerves. So subtle and poisonous is the Narcissistic variant of sadism that it might well be regarded as the most dangerous of all." [3]

Read on to see how Vaknin describes how to conduct yourself if you choose to stay in a relationship with someone like this:

"You will be required to deny your self: your hopes, your dreams, your fears, your aspirations, your sexual needs, your emotional needs, and sometimes your material needs. You will be asked to deny reality and ignore it. It is very disorientating. Most victims feel that they are going crazy or that they are guilty of something obscure, opaque, and ominous. It is Kafkaesque: an endless, on-going trial without clear laws, known procedures, and identified judges. It is nightmarish. " [4]

What are they like with children?

As you now know, narcissists will never let their guard down enough with anyone to ever feel genuine love for them nor do they experience real emotions. Therefore, doing things for others whom they have no feelings for is pointless. Even their own children pose a threat to them. Children talk back and do not always agree.

Narcissists only enjoy being around their children when the child is a shining example of them or when the child does exactly what is asked of them. Since children cannot be on their best behavior 100 percent of the time, I'm sure you can imagine how a narcissistic parent responds to their children on a daily basis.

The majority of the time, narcissists are either jealous of the attention their child receives from their partner and others, or they are frustrated by the amount of time and energy the child requires of them. Since narcissists do not enjoy expending energy or doing things for others unless they get something out of it, they have very little tolerance for the needs and demands of children. There is no immediate gratification for a narcissist after tending to the needs of a child. Their whole life is about fulfilling their own needs, not others'.

A narcissist's biggest fear in life is to find himself in a mediocre, monotonous existence. Narcissists feel omnipotent, grandiose, and unique. To live a routine, common, domestic life terrifies them. What is important to understand is that a narcissist will inevitably pull away, disappear or run at some point to avoid the dreaded idea of being settled-down for life.

Why are we drawn to them?

If you're like me, you have fallen for more than one narcissist. As a result, I often ask myself why I'm attracted to these personality types and would like to understand why they are attracted to me. The first part of this question is simple. As I mentioned earlier, it is easy to fall for them. They are charming, witty and often the life of the party. To spend time with them is exciting and fun. There is an intensity about them that is indescribable. They possess a force that is magnetic. There is simply never a dull moment and they always keep you on your toes.

On the other hand, understanding why they are attracted to me is a bit more perplexing. Recently, however, I have finally started to understand it. I have learned I am an *Empath*, which describes a person who is highly tuned into other's emotions and extremely sensitive. I have always been this way. In fact, my childhood friend was once asked to describe me in one word and without hesitation she responded by saying "SENSITIVE." I was surprised by the rapid-fire response she gave, but it was eye-opening, to say the least.

I have always been sensitive, and I find this to be both a blessing and a curse. I can feel other people's emotions as if they're my own. I have been told by others that my ability to empathize with them is palpable. While this is a blessing in many ways, it can prove difficult in interpersonal relationships. *Empaths* feel things more strongly than others and narcissists pick up on the sensitivity of an *Empath* and take advantage of it. An *Empath* is the perfect accoutrement to a narcissist.

Empaths are incredible listeners, naturally giving and always there for people they care about. Narcissists notice this immediately because they purposefully seek a partner who is compassionate and in tune with their never-ending needs. An *Empath* absorbs the emotions of others and will easily fall prey to a narcissist, who uses others as an emotional sponge.

Empaths are very sensitive to suffering in the world and are often idealists who want to fix the world's problems. *Empaths* have an incredible capacity for self-sacrifice and are often found volunteering or dedicating time to help others. People naturally feel comfortable sharing their feelings with an *Empath* because of their incredible ability to feel compassion and connect with others.

Whereas a narcissist does not connect well with others, an *Empath* connects too much. When *Empaths* are around peace and love, they flourish. However, when surrounded by an emotional vampire, like the narcissist, an *Empath* is ravaged. An *Empath* absorbs the negativity, fear and rage of a narcissist. So much so that they take on these problems as their own and try to fix things for their partner. This is precisely what a narcissist is looking for in a partner and exactly why they seek out relationships with *Empaths.*

They chose us for a reason. They chose us because we are strong, successful, intelligent and driven. They need someone to take care of them and certainly are not going to choose someone who can't provide for them. They know they can take a lot from us and gain significantly by being in a relationship with us. They want to be taken care of and choose strong people to partner with for a reason. Overall, I believe being an *Empath* is truly a gift, but we must be careful not to allow others to take advantage of us.

Do they miss us?

As long as a narcissist has someone to cater to his needs and stroke his ego, he does not miss us. A narcissist does not experience emotions the way we do. Our memories are triggered by our five senses. Narcissists have little to no emotion so their memory recall is much different than ours.

There are two types of memory for the same situation. One is explicit memory - a memory of the details of the experience and the other is

implicit memory - a memory of the emotions connected to the experience. For example, smelling a baked apple pie reminds me of my beloved grandmother's wonderful baking and brings about an emotional response of missing her. This is what we call implicit memory or emotional memory.

Explicit memory, on the other hand, is different and includes my ability to remember how to make the pie - the details of the experience.

Narcissists are very good at explicit memory - the details, the how to, when, where, what, etc. However, they have horrible implicit memory, which is always triggered by an emotion, or sense of smell, touch, taste, etc. They are incapable of bringing forth emotional memories, only factual memories. Therefore, if you wonder whether they have memories of us, the answer is yes and no.

Yes, they remember the details of your relationship with them. However, the emotions of it are totally lost on them. They enjoyed their time with you. Trust me, you made them feel alive. If not, they never would have chosen you. However, they are incapable of feeling any real emotion and certainly will not experience emotions when remembering you. I know it's hard to accept, but it is simply the way they are built.

Why do they keep coming back?

Why do they keep coming back? Why can't they leave us alone? It is important to remind you that a narcissist has no inner-sense of self. As you know, they disconnected from themselves a long time ago. Because they have no sense of self, they must be validated by others in order to feel alive. Without outside validation, they feel dead inside.

If a narcissist is feeling insecure or lonely, he will seek out validation from anyone he can get it from. If he comes back to you after your relationship has ended, you must understand he is coming to you because he is not getting enough attention or validation from his current source of Narcissistic Supply. I know this is tough to accept, but it is true. He is not returning to you because he misses you or genuinely loves you. If he returns to you, it is simply because he needs to be validated and nothing more.

If he can't get a positive reaction from you, he will ensure he can elicit a negative reaction. This is precisely why he comes back to insult or demean you. All he needs is a reaction from you - good or bad. He doesn't care if it is a positive or negative reaction as long as he gets a reaction from you. He needs to know he still has some kind of hold or effect on you.

Please remember, a narcissist is only returning to get a *quick fix* on his addiction to Narcissistic Supply. He desperately needs outside validation and will do anything to secure it. Whether it be upsetting you to get a rise out of you or charming you into submission, he is determined to get a reaction from you at that moment.

Once you validate him by responding to him in any way, shape or form, he has gotten his fix and will move on to the next best high.

Getting a reaction out of you is like a drug to him. He gets off on it and needs it in order to thrive. It gives him a thrill.

Please do not give him this satisfaction. Please do not feed his addiction. The only way to deal with a narcissist is to go *No Contact,* which we will discuss later in the book. Just remember, indifference is the only way to respond to his attempts to get a reaction from you. I hope if you understand why he is coming back, you will be able to stay away from him. Do not give in to him. He is just looking for a *quick fix* and will immediately move on once he has used you for it.

Why is it so hard for us to stay away?

Many of us don't understand why we can't stay away from them even after we learn how toxic they are to us. We must remember they have brainwashed us. Like a salesman, they keep us coming back with the lure, the promise and the hook.

They are master manipulators. They know how to make us feel guilty,

38

so we will come back for absolution. They know how to make us feel sorry for them, so we will offer to help them. They know how to promise great things, so we will return in hopes that it will be different this time.

They know how to make us doubt ourselves, so we will seek validation from them. Ultimately, they have trained us to return to them over and over again.

There is a principle in behaviorism called *Random Reinforcement*, which explains how inconsistent responses to identical behavior can lead to addiction. This same principle is precisely why slot machines and gambling are dangerously addictive. You get a big reward for a certain behavior on one occasion; other times that same behavior leads to a huge loss or punishment.

The thrill that the next go-around might be the big pay-off or reward for a certain behavior keeps us coming back for more. We chase that high from the last time we were rewarded. Being in a relationship with a narcissist is like a roller-coaster ride with incredible highs and unbelievable lows. It is exhilarating and exciting one moment, and demoralizing and demeaning the next.

We get caught in a cycle of chasing that next high, hoping that if we weather the storm, the next moment will bring the return of the good again. Unfortunately, the good never returns permanently. The narcissist knows by rewarding us intermittently, we remain hooked. They keep us on our toes guessing and always ensure we are left wanting more from them.

Narcissists are brilliant manipulators and know what they're doing every step of the way. They enjoy punishing us more than they enjoy rewarding us. It is all part of a master plan to keep us under their control. It is part of the lure (the hook) and they use it to play us like pawns.

After spending years with a narcissist, we begin to doubt our ability to make decisions. They have controlled and directed our every move for years. They train and condition us to look to them for answers, which ultimately strips us of our ability to make any choices for ourselves. As a result, we are terrified of being alone.

Stockholm Syndrome is a term used to describe a psychological phenomenon where hostages bond with their captors. The syndrome is named after the Norrmalmstorg robbery of Kreditbanken at Norrmalmstorg in Stockholm where bank robbers held bank employees hostage from August 23 to August 28, 1973.

In this case, the victims became emotionally attached to their captors and even defended them after they were released. The term *Stockholm Syndrome* was coined by the criminologist and psychiatrist Nils Bejerot who assisted the police during the robbery. Frank Ochberg originally defined it to aid in the management of hostage situations and describes it as:

"A primitive gratitude for the gift of life."

There is still debate as to what specific factors contribute to the development of *Stockholm Syndrome*, but the goal of every abuser is the same – to ensure the victim becomes reliant and dependent on him for survival. Continued contact between the perpetrator and the hostage, a long duration before resolution and emotional abuse vs. physical abuse are key components. These are the very components at play when in a long-term relationship with a narcissist, which helps explain why it is so difficult for us to stay away.

Narcissists isolate us from our family and friends so we become dependent on them. As discussed earlier, they use various methods of coercion, including *gaslighting* to cause us to doubt ourselves and become reliant on them.

Stockholm Syndrome makes it very hard for us to break off contact.

Because the narcissist has brainwashed us to be reliant on him for survival and the truth, we are afraid to be on our own.

This is often referred to as *Trauma Bonding* because the narcissist has conditioned us to believe we can't live without him. He wants to keep us confused and coming back to him so he can keep using us forever. It takes a lot of time and effort for us to finally realize we are actually better off on our own.

It is for this reason our support forum at
www.ThePathForwardNow.com
is so important when coming out
of a relationship with a narcissist.

We need to deprogram from the narcissist and talk to others who understand what we are going through. No one understands like those who have been through it themselves and the support we give one another is essential.

CHAPTER 2

STEP TWO
GET IT OUT

We find an outlet to share and express our emotions.

As humans, we absolutely must process our feelings before we can recover or heal from any painful experience. Until we do this, we remain stuck. This is not only important for our emotional health, but our physical health as well.

We Gotta Get It Out!

Research now exists to prove that unresolved emotional pain can cause physical illness. I had such a severe auto-immune response after my divorce that I lost the ability to walk for one month. It was a terrifying experience and proved beyond a shadow of a doubt that my emotional health is directly linked to my physical health. Hence the importance of processing our feelings before they become toxic. What we now know is that unresolved emotional trauma floods our bodies with hormones, which leave our immune systems weak and vulnerable to attack.

People tell us to just move on and expect us to get over it, but we can't until we fully process how we feel about it, share our story with others who can relate, and organize our thoughts in such a way that we feel we have made sense of the situation.

You may ask: "How do you make sense of a senseless situation?"

Well, this is certainly not easy, but I believe sorting out our feelings and organizing our thoughts in a way that helps us feel we have given the experience some kind of form and structure helps tremendously. We have a need to organize the trauma and chaos we experience in life.

It makes us feel better to express ourselves in a way that allows us to feel as though we can finally put the whole crazy mess to rest in our

44

heads. Until we do this, we will always obsess about it. Each of us must find an outlet to give creative expression and form to what we experienced. For me, this outlet has been my first book, *It's All About Him* and my music CD, *Gotta Get It Out.*

The key is to find an outlet in which we can express our feelings and share our story. For some, this may include talking to family members or friends, sharing on our on-line forum, journaling or creating art or music. Whatever it is, it is critical that you find an outlet to express yourself in a way that helps you release your emotions and put things in perspective. In my opinion, it is the only way to put it to rest in your mind.

A narcissist will never give us closure, but we can help ourselves get closure by making sure we process our feelings. Why is this step so critical? Research tells us the main reason for the stress of psychological trauma is that our memories of these horrible events are fragmented. Psychologically traumatic events are ones that have no good explanation. You have painful facts that make no sense, right?

Our natural tendency is to avoid thinking about painful memories or events. We suppress them and hope they will go away. But, they don't. If you don't process them, deal with them and get them out, they will never go away. This is because the mind is most settled when there is coherence to our thoughts.

The only way to resolve conflicting thoughts is by remembering them, processing them and making sense of them. One way of doing this is by sharing our story with others. Sharing our story with people who understand is extremely healing and cathartic. It validates our experience and reassures us that we are not alone in our struggle.

Telling your story allows you to link together your emotional memories, which makes the traumatic events more coherent. It makes memories of these events less likely to be repeatedly called to mind so they can be laid to rest. This stage is imperative before you can move on.

Do not be afraid to cry as often as you need. It is cathartic and necessary in order for you to move on. Do not be afraid to get angry... that's your self-esteem returning and you can channel it into doing things for yourself to help you heal. Too often people think anger is a negative emotion. Anger is not inherently positive or negative. It is how we RESPOND to our anger that determines whether it is positive or negative.

We cannot control what happens to us in life, but we can control how we RESPOND to it. It is our response that determines our future.

Taking steps to take care of yourself is a positive response to anger. Do not be afraid to feel your feelings and get honest with yourself. Remember, we must get *real to heal*. If you repress your feelings, you will remain stuck. Be gentle with yourself and grateful that you have the ability to feel. When you feel, you know you're alive, right? I would rather feel pain and know I'm alive than feel nothing. The one thing a narcissist can never take away from us is our ability to feel. A narcissist will never experience the range of emotions we do, which is precisely why they are so jealous, envious and covetous of those of us who can.

Share Your Story

Today we now have proof that writing is therapeutic. James Pennebaker, PhD., a psychologist and researcher, has conducted studies that show improvement in immune system functioning and emotional well-being

46

when research participants write about difficult or traumatic events in their lives. When you share your story, you no longer feel alone or isolated. You feel connected and understood.

"I will write myself into well-being." ~ *Nancy Mair*

As Louise DeSalvo points out in her powerful book, "Writing as a Way of Healing," many writers, like Virginia Woolf and Henry Miller describe their work as a form of analysis or therapy. Before treatment was available, many writers used their work in this way. Writing allows us to release pent-up feelings that otherwise may not have come to the surface by talking. I know this is certainly the case for me. I find writing to be incredibly healing.

I love the way DeSalvo describes the therapeutic process of writing:

"We receive a shock or a blow or experience trauma in our lives. In exploring it, examining it, and putting it into words, we stop seeing it as a random, unexplained event. We begin to understand the order behind appearances.

Expressing it in language robs the event of its power to hurt us; it also assuages our pain. And by expressing ourselves in language, by examining these shocks, we paradoxically experience delight – pleasure, even – which comes from the discoveries we make as we write, from the order we create from seeming randomness or chaos.

Ultimately, then, writing about difficulties enables us to discover the wholeness of things, the connectedness of human experience. We understand that our greatest shocks do not separate us from humankind. Instead, through expressing ourselves, we establish our connection with others and with the world."[1]

47

Sharing your story with others on our forum who know exactly what you're going through is extremely healing. It's comforting to know you are not alone and that others can relate to your confusion and pain. Remember, the narcissist wants us to doubt ourselves and our sense of reality. By talking to others on our site who know the tactics these men play, you can help prevent yourself from getting sucked back in by the narcissist. Being connected to others who "get it" is extremely helpful during those times when you are feeling weak and want to see him or talk to him.

Your first writing assignment is to put your story into words. Please obtain a notepad or diary that you will use as your own personal *Recovery Journal*. It can be as fancy or as simple as you would like it to be, but be sure you designate something that is strictly for the purpose of your recovery and nothing else. Throughout the book, you will use your *Recovery Journal* for various writing assignments in order to help you process your feelings and heal.

Write about your relationship with your narcissist. Do not worry about grammar or punctuation. Focus instead on documenting the series of events in your relationship and most importantly, the feelings you experienced. You can do this privately in your *Recovery Journal*, anonymously under the *Share Your Story* section on our on-line forum or both. You will be amazed at what you learn about your relationship with your narcissist and more importantly, your relationship with yourself as a result of putting your experience into words.

The Importance of Feeling

We must allow ourselves to feel. Often times, when in the midst of a breakup or divorce, we do not take the time to feel our feelings. That is because when you experience trauma, you are often in survival mode.

You're trying to keep it together for your children and/or other family members. All your energy is focused on getting through the transition. It is natural not to grieve while in survival mode. It is all a process. That is why it is so important to work *The Six Steps* to ensure you deal with your feelings now instead of being forced to deal with them in the future when you are not prepared.

Many people, especially men are socialized to believe that we shouldn't cry or exhibit our emotions in any way, shape or form. We learn to repress our feelings as if they are a sign of insecurity or weakness. In my opinion, this is disastorous to our well-being.

Primal Scream Therapy is a **trauma**-based **psychotherapy** created by **Arthur Janov**, who believes **neurosis** is caused by the **repressed** pain of childhood trauma. Janov argues that unresolved pain can be brought to conscious awareness by re-experiencing painful childhood feelings or events and fully expressing the resulting pain during therapy. Janov believes this type of therapy resolves pain from the past. Primal therapy first became influential in the early 1970s, after the publication of Janov's first book, "**The Primal Scream.**"

Janov used *Primal Scream Therapy* to help patients resolve childhood pain by processing their emotions, integrating them and thus, becoming *real*. The goal of his therapy is to lessen or eliminate the hold early trauma exerts on adult life.

As we know, trauma can be experienced at any point in one's life. In a relationship with a narcissist, emotional abuse causes trauma. Emotional abuse is much harder to pinpoint than physical abuse because there are no visible scars. However, emotional abuse is just as real as any other type of abuse and causes the same kind of emotional trauma. The resulting trauma you experienced cannot be ignored. Just like a physical wound, it must be dealt with and tended to in order to heal.

Janov states that neurosis is the result of suppressed pain, which is the result of trauma. According to Janov, the only way to reverse neurosis is for the patient to confront their trauma and express the emotions that occurred at that time. I agree and believe that we must confront these experiences and process our feelings about what occurred in order to move on.

John Lennon's *Primal Scream Therapy* sessions with Arthur Janov in 1970 were the catalyst in Lennon's most emotionally bare album, "John Lennon/Plastic Ono Band". I love what Lennon had to say about *Primal Scream Therapy* in this Howard Smith Radio Interview:

"There's no way of describing it, it all sounds so straight just talking about it, what you actually do is cry. Instead of penting up emotion, or pain, feel it rather than putting it away for some rainy day..... I think everybody's blocked, I haven't met anybody that isn't a complete blockage of pain from childhood, from birth on...... It's like somewhere along the line we were switched off not to feel things, like for instance, crying, men crying and women being very girlish or whatever it is, somewhere you have to switch into a role and this therapy gives you back the switch, locate it and switch back into feeling just as a human being, not as a male or a female or as a famous person or not famous person, they switch you back to being a baby and therefore you feel as a child does, but it's something we forget because there's so much pressure and pain and whatever it is that is life, everyday life, that we gradually switch off over the years. All the generation gap crap is that the older people are more dead, as the years go by the pain doesn't go away, the pain of living, you have to kill yourself to survive. This allows you to live and survive without killing yourself."

It is critical for you to confront the trauma you experienced and process the emotions that are a direct result of the pain you endured. We cannot repress our feelings and we must confront what happened to us. If we do not, we will remain stuck.

"There is no coming to consciousness without pain." ~ Carl Jung

I spent many years in this state, which I refer to as my *dark period*. Eckhart Tolle refers to this state of being as the *pain body*. In his groundbreaking book, "The Power of Now," Tolle explains how the *pain body* is actually afraid of the light of consciousness. Its survival is dependent on your unconscious fear of facing the pain that lives inside you.

In other words, you will remain in a state of pain, darkness or unhappiness as long as you continue to lie to yourself and deny your reality. Resistance is what keeps us stuck in the unconscious realm. Tolle believes the more you resist the present moment, the more pain you create within yourself.[2]

In my opinion, the only true path to enlightenment is to drop all inner resistance and be honest with ourselves. We must allow ourselves to feel our feelings and not be ashamed. When you give a feeling full expression, it diminishes its power and brings about a transformation. Once you acknowledge and express the feeling, it causes the feeling to subside, as it can't go on forever.

We must not be afraid to cry. It is an emotional release, which is good for us. Poets have known this for years:

"To weep is to make less the depth of grief."
~ William Shakespeare

"Heaven knows we need never be ashamed of our tears, for they are rain upon the blinding dust of earth, overlying our hard hearts." ~ Charles Dickens

Fortunately, science is now confirming such statements. Recent research confirms that crying is good for us because it cleanses our system of toxins and waste, reduces tension and increases our body's ability to heal itself.

Alan Wolfelt Ph.D., a professor at the University of Colorado Medical School, has measured the chemical benefits of crying and states:

"In my clinical experience with thousands of mourners, I have observed changes in physical (appearance) following the expression of tears...Not only do people feel better after crying ; they also look better."

The kind of tears our eyes produce for moisture to remove dust or sand and the kind that we produce by crying are chemically different. Crying tears are made-up of manganese. In fact, crying tears are thirty times richer in manganese than blood is, for example. According to biochemists, manganese is only one of three chemicals that are stored up by stress and flushed out by a good cry.

In the school of nursing at Marquette University, nurses are asked not to immediately provide tranquilizers to weeping patients. Instead, they are encouraged to allow the tears to do their own therapeutic work. Dr. Margaret Crepeau, professor of nursing at Marquette states:

"Laughter and tears are two inherent natural medicines whereby we can reduce duress, let out negative feelings and recharge. They truly are the body's own best resources."

Studies find that men die sooner than women after any major stressful or traumatic experience. A man's refusal to feel his feelings and his determination to repress emotions is thought to contribute to this statistic, which lends further support to my belief that we *Gotta Get it Out* in order to heal.

Letter to the Narcissist

Your next writing assignment will further your ability to feel your feelings. You should now write a letter to your narcissist. As mentioned, a narcissist will never give us closure, but we can give ourselves closure by processing our feelings and allowing ourselves to feel the emotions we need to feel.

You can say anything you want in your letter. It is your letter to your narcissist to get your feelings out. You will never send this letter to him, of course. It is simply for your benefit only. It should come from your heart and has no specific requirements. You should tell your narcissist how he hurt you. Tell him how you feel. Explain what you sacrificed and what he didn't. Don't hold back. Get it all out. This is the time to tell him everything you ever wanted to and more.

Now, please share this letter with someone by reading it aloud. This person can be a family member, a close friend, a therapist, a life coach or a member of our forum. Read the letter with conviction and authority and allow yourself to feel your feelings. You will most likely feel like crying or screaming as you read your letter aloud. Do not hold back. Allow yourself to feel your feelings.

Letter from the Narcissist

Next, you should write a letter to yourself from your narcissist. You will be writing this letter as if you are your narcissist and you are finally realizing the error of your ways. A narcissist will never come around, but that doesn't mean we can't facilitate the words we need to hear in order to move on. If we wait for them to say these things, we will be waiting for eternity. In the letter, your narcissist is saying goodbye to you and telling you everything you always wanted to hear.

Write the letter you have always fantasized about receiving from your narcissist. In the letter, your narcissist should acknowledge and apologize for his behavior. Have someone else read this letter aloud to you. Even though your narcissist is not saying it, the effect of hearing the words you've needed to hear for months, years or even decades is powerful and healing. The communication that occurs on a subconscious level will make a difference.

We must process and validate our feelings before we can move on. Repressing our feelings has been shown to negatively affect our physical and emotional health. It is absolutely critical to process our feelings if we want to improve our happiness and well-being.

CHAPTER 3

STEP THREE
NO CONTACT

We accept the only way to restore our sanity and regain control of our lives is through *No Contact.*

The only way to break free from a narcissist is to establish and maintain a rule of *No Contact* with him. You must treat him as if you are breaking a toxic drug habit. You must realize that he has become like a drug to you. Just as he needs others to validate his existence, he has now programmed you to believe you need him in order to survive. You must understand that you are addicted to him right now, but this is only temporary and a direct result of being brainwashed.

A narcissist programs you to question yourself....question everything you do, in fact. This is his goal from the very beginning. He knows if he can cause you to doubt yourself, you will become dependent on him for validation and keep coming back. It is critical that you understand you will never get over a narcissist if you go back or remain in contact with him in any way or capacity. You can and will deprogram from him, but only if you establish *No Contact*. You must cut off all contact with him in order to break free.

No Contact means just that.....you must have absolutely **NO CONTACT** with your narcissist. In other words:

No personal visits

No phone calls, incoming or outgoing.

Do not answer his calls.

Block his phone number.

If he uses a different number and you do answer, hang up immediately.

No emails, incoming or outgoing. Delete before reading.

No texts, incoming or outgoing. Delete before reading.

No Facebook, MySpace or dating websites where he may be found.

Do not look for him on the Internet.

Do not Google his name.

Do not talk to his friends or family. Avoid these conversations at all costs.

Delete and destroy any reminders of him.

Do not save emails, letters or photos. Everything must go!

The act of cleaning or disposing of certain articles is internally cleansing. It helps clear away the memories associated with the relationship. Remove tangible reminders of your narcissist, such as framed photos or albums. This will help you "cut the chords" of connection, so to speak. It is the connection that is so intense. They have their hooks in us deep. Any physical or visual exercise you can perform to help you cut off your connection with your narcissist is one I highly recommend.

A narcissist will contact you with the hope that you will return in a state of panic because he has led you to believe you cannot exist on your own. He wants to convince you that you need him in order to survive. The irony in all of this is that the narcissist is the one who needs YOU in order to feel alive, but he has done a brilliant job of PROJECTING his issues onto you so you are the one who feels dependent on him.

Clearly, when one is co-parenting with a narcissist, *No Contact* is somewhat tricky. Where children are involved, the goal of *No Contact* is to refrain from engaging in any type of communication with him above and beyond what is necessary for your children's well-being. Aside from this, you should not have any contact with him whatsoever. He has already taken enough from you. Do not continue to let him take more. Your days of being the doormat and servant to the narcissist are over.

Please remember, *No Contact* is the only way to begin the process of deprogramming from a narcissist. Unless we physically detach and disconnect from a narcissist, he will ALWAYS control us.

"You cannot solve a problem from the same consciousness that created it." ~ Albert Einstein

Having any type of contact with the narcissist while trying to break free will only keep you stuck under his spell. Creating distance is the only way to gain perspective and see things as they truly are. We must break contact in order to really assess the situation. It is this distance that allows us to look at things from the perspective of a "PLAYER" considering their next move versus a "PAWN" waiting to be played.

We often do not realize how horribly they treated us until we physically remove ourselves from their proximity. Any contact with them keeps us under their influence, which makes it more difficult to recognize what is going on. It is only once we pull away completely and deprogram that we begin to see the extent of the emotional abuse we suffered. We are amazed by what we tolerated. This just goes to show how strongly brainwashed we were.

While they do a very good job of brainwashing us into believing we need them, we must remember that we are NOT reliant on them for survival.

They have only manipulated us into believing this is the case. We have the ability to get in touch with ourselves again. They do not. We cannot let them drag us down into their miserable world of nonexistence. The longer we are in contact with them, the longer it takes to deprogram from them. The only way to successfully start to deprogram is to establish *No Contact* as soon as possible.

Cognitive Dissonance

When coming out of a relationship with a narcissist, our minds are experiencing severe *Cognitive Dissonance*, which is the difficulty of trying to hold two opposing thoughts or beliefs at the same time. Cigarette smokers are a perfect example of individuals who may experience *Cognitive Dissonance*. They enjoy their habit, but at the same time, loathe it because they know it is bad for them, right?

Cognitive Dissonance leads to obsessive thought because we are trying to make sense of a situation that makes no sense. How can I love something that I also hate? How can I be crazy in love with this person, but despise him at the same time? We remember the wonderful times, the good times and the person we thought we fell in love with and we miss him. We wonder what happened to him. Where did he go? Why did he disappear? What did I do wrong?

While we're remembering this person who no longer seems to exist, we are grappling with a new person we no longer recognize, and we don't know how to feel about him. How can he be good and bad? How can I love him and hate him? Trying to resolve this in our minds is very confusing and leads to *Cognitive Dissonance*, which causes obsessive, intrusive thoughts that impede our ability to concentrate, work, sleep, eat or function.

We must remember that we did NOTHING wrong nor is there anything that can be done to bring this person back to us. The person we fell in love with is not who we thought he was at all. He never existed. We fell in love with an illusion. Narcissists are shallow, hollow and empty.

Realizing this person is NOT who you thought he was and NOT someone you want to be with is KEY to maintaining *No Contact*.

Once you realize separation from the narcissist is a GOOD THING, you are on the path to true recovery.

My ex-husband's favorite poem was "The Hollow Men" by T.S. Eliot, and I think it tells us all we need to know about these personalities in order to stay away.

The Hollow Men by T.S. Eliot

We are the hollow men
We are the stuffed men
Leaning together
Headpiece filled with straw. Alas!
Our dried voices, when
We whisper together
Are quiet and meaningless
As wind in dry grass
Or rats' feet over broken glass
In our dry cellar

Shape without form, shade without color,
Paralyzed force, gesture without motion;
Those who have crossed
With direct eyes, to death's other Kingdom

Remember us -- if at all -- not as lost
Violent souls, but only
As the hollow men
The stuffed men.

II

Eyes I dare not meet in dreams
In death's dream kingdom
These do not appear:
There, the eyes are
Sunlight on a broken column
There, is a tree swinging
And voices are
In the wind's singing
More distant and more solemn
Than a fading star.

Let me be no nearer
In death's dream kingdom
Let me also wear
Such deliberate disguises
Rat's coat, crowskin, crossed staves
In a field
Behaving as the wind behaves
No nearer --

Not that final meeting
In the twilight kingdom

III

This is the dead land
This is cactus land

Here the stone images
Are raised, here they receive
The supplication of a dead man's hand
Under the twinkle of a fading star.

Is it like this
In death's other kingdom
Waking alone
At the hour when we are
Trembling with tenderness
Lips that would kiss
Form prayers to broken stone.

IV

The eyes are not here
There are no eyes here
In this valley of dying stars
In this hollow valley
This broken jaw of our lost kingdoms

In this last of meeting places
We grope together
And avoid speech
Gathered on this beach of the tumid river

Sightless, unless
The eyes reappear
As the perpetual star
Multifoliate rose
Of death's twilight kingdom
The hope only
Of empty men.

V

Here we go round the prickly pear
Prickly pear prickly pear
Here we go round the prickly pear
At five o'clock in the morning.

Between the idea
And the reality
Between the motion
And the act
Falls the Shadow

For Thine is the Kingdom

Between the conception
And the creation
Between the emotion
And the response
Falls the Shadow

Life is very long

Between the desire
And the spasm
Between the potency
And the existence
Between the essence
And the descent
Falls the Shadow

For Thine is the Kingdom

For Thine is

Life is

For Thine is the

This is the way the world ends
This is the way the world ends
This is the way the world ends
Not with a bang but a whimper.

Once we learn to see the narcissist for the person he really is, we are finally able to free ourselves.

<u>**Obsessive Thoughts**</u>

When coming out of a relationship with a narcissist, it is normal to experience obsessive thoughts. This is because we have been brainwashed to doubt ourselves and become reliant on our narcissist for the truth. We have also been conditioned in life to avoid pain and seek pleasure. As a result, we enage in obsessive thinking so we can avoid confronting the painful reality of our situation. We use the recurring thoughts to distract ourselves from what we really need to confront and process – our feelings!

Many of us avoid our feelings by identifying too much with our mind - we over-analyze and over-think everything. I know I am guilty of this, and *Cognitive Dissonance* contributes to this phenomenon. What we don't realize is that we are unconsciously obsessing in an attempt to avoid our pain. Instead of allowing ourselves to feel, we distract ourselves by getting caught up in obsessive ideation.

Obsessive thoughts are a reaction to anxiety that we feel. No one likes to feel anxiety, so we find ways to numb or decrease our anxiety. One way we do this is through engaging in obsessive compulsive behavior.

Just as one uses drugs or alcohol, one can use obsessive thoughts to avoid having to feel.

It took me a long time to figure this out, but when I did, it really opened my eyes. By obsessing, overanalyzing and staying "in our head" we avoid having to really feel the emotions that are trying to pour out of us. Believe it or not, this is exactly what the narcissist is counting on. They want us to disconnect from ourselves so we remain dependent on them for survival.

When all we can do is obsess about our narcissist, it is near impossible to avoid responding when we hear from him. We become consumed with trying to figure him out. Although we have the knowledge we need to stay away, *Cognitive Dissonance* keeps us wondering if he is really all that bad. We want to give him another chance to prove us wrong, to prove that he really is capable of love.

Unfortunately, we learn the hard way that he will never change. Some of us need to learn this lesson more than once. Others can move on more quickly. It is my hope that by understanding why you obsess about him, it will help you stay away and move on more quickly.

Please remember when you are stuck in an obsessive-compulsive cycle of thought, you are trying to avoid having to feel. By distracting yourself with mind rituals, you can easily forget all about the emotions trying to surface inside you. Think about it, if you are engaged in obsessive thought and consumed with your mind, who has time to feel? Identifying with your mind allows you to avoid having to feel.

If you find yourself obsessing, I challenge you to ask yourself this question:

"What feeling am I trying to avoid right now?"

I guarantee you will find that there is a very strong emotion you are avoiding. We have to stop being afraid to feel our feelings. We must learn not to elude our feelings with methods of distraction.

The importance of feeling is something we will discuss in more detail in a later chapter. For now, just remember, if you catch yourself obsessing, stop and ask yourself what it is you are feeling at the moment. You will be surprised by what you learn.

Post-Traumatic Stress Disorder

Along with *Cognitive Dissonance*, you should be aware of the possibility that you may be suffering from Post-traumatic Stress Disorder (PTSD) as a result of the emotional abuse and psychological trauma you endured in your relationship with a narcissist.

According to the DSM-IV, PTSD occurs when:

A. The person has been exposed to a traumatic event in which both of the following have been present:

(1) the person experienced, witnessed, or was confronted with an event or events that involved actual or threatened death or serious injury, or a threat to the physical integrity of self or others

(2) the person's response involved intense fear, helplessness, or horror. Note: In children, this may be expressed instead by disorganized or agitated behavior.

B. The traumatic event is persistently re-experienced in one (or more) of the following ways:

(1) recurrent and intrusive distressing recollections of the event, including images, thoughts, or perceptions. Note: In young children, repetitive play may occur in which themes or aspects of the trauma are expressed.

(2) recurrent distressing dreams of the event. Note: In children, there may be frightening dreams without recognizable content.

(3) acting or feeling as if the traumatic event were recurring (includes a sense of reliving the experience, illusions, hallucinations, and dissociative flashback episodes, including those that occur upon awakening or when intoxicated). Note: In young children, trauma-specific reenactment may occur.

(4) intense psychological distress at exposure to internal or external cues that symbolize or resemble an aspect of the traumatic event.

(5) physiological reactivity on exposure to internal or external cues that symbolize or resemble an aspect of the traumatic event.

C. Persistent avoidance of stimuli associated with the trauma and numbing of general responsiveness (not present before the trauma), as indicated by three (or more) of the following:

(1) efforts to avoid thoughts, feelings, or conversations associated with the trauma

(2) efforts to avoid activities, places, or people that arouse recollections of the trauma

(3) inability to recall an important aspect of the trauma

(4) markedly diminished interest or participation in significant activities

(5) feeling of detachment or estrangement from others

(6) restricted range of affect (e.g., unable to have loving feelings)

(7) sense of a foreshortened future (e.g., does not expect to have a career, marriage, children, or a normal life span)

D. Persistent symptoms of increased arousal (not present before the trauma), as indicated by two (or more) of the following:

(1) difficulty falling or staying asleep
(2) irritability or outbursts of anger
(3) difficulty concentrating
(4) hypervigilance
(5) exaggerated startle response

E. Duration of the disturbance (symptoms in Criteria B, C, and D) is more than one month.

F. The disturbance causes clinically significant distress or impairment in social, occupational, or other important areas of functioning.

Specify if:
Acute: if duration of symptoms is less than 3 months
Chronic: if duration of symptoms is 3 months or more

With Delayed Onset: if onset of symptoms is at least 6 months after the stressor

PTSD is very serious and can be detrimental to your physical health if not treated. If you feel you are experiencing any of these symptoms, it is critical you seek medical attention right away. No matter how much effort you put into your recovery program, if you are suffering from PTSD, it will prohibit you from making any progress whatsoever. Only a doctor can determine if you are experiencing PTSD and provide the proper medical attention you need in order to heal and move on.

Hoovering

During the *No Contact* phase, you should be aware of a technique called *Hoovering*, which the narcissist will use in an attempt to win you back. According to the on-line Urban Dictionary, the definition of *Hoovering* is:

"Being manipulated back into a relationship with threats of suicide, self-harm, or threats of false criminal accusations. Relationship manipulation often associated with individuals suffering from personality disorders like Borderline Personality Disorder or Narcissistic Personality Disorder."

It is important to be mindful of this occurring so you can recognize it and not get *sucked-in*. The term *Hoovering* gets its name from the Hoover vacuum. The narcissist uses all kinds of manipulative behavior to *suck you back in* to the relationship. He may threaten suicide saying that he can't live without you. He purposefully plays on your good-naturedness to get you to feel sorry for him.

During this stage, the narcissist reverts back to the courting behavior he exhibited in the beginning of your relationship in order to win you back. He acts loving, compassionate and supportive. He promises you everything you ever wanted and more. He acknowledges the error of his ways and promises to change.

Narcissists are very charming so the initial *Hoovering* stage is often quite successful. Not to mention, the narcissist knows you well enough to know which buttons to push to get you to succumb to him.

Please know that the minute you take him back, he will revert to his old behavior. He is only coming back to you because he is incapable of being alone. He needs someone in his life to validate him at all times.

Anyone who has taken a narcissist back can attest to the fact that they quickly revert to their old behavior once they have you back under their control. I encourage anyone looking for proof of this to visit our on-line forum. There is not one story of someone taking a narcissist back who changed for the better. Every time you take him back, you only end up hurting yourself and prolonging your pain. Narcissists are incapable of change. *No Contact* is the only way to go when breaking free.

NarcSpeak

Narcissists say the strangest things... and we are often left scratching our heads - trying to make sense of the senseless.

Remember, narcissists are not normal. They don't think like we do. They don't speak normally either. Most of what they say is meant to confuse us, throw us off and manipulate us. They use backward-talk, projection, martyrdom and almost ALWAYS provoke us to respond in a manner they can then use against us. They often use NLP = NeuroLinguistic Programming - used in sales, marketing, politics and seduction/mind control. They are brilliant manipulators.

As such, it is critical you are aware of this tactic so you can recognize when it is occurring.

Below are common narcissistic comments that we have translated on our on-line forum at **www.ThePathForwardNow.com**.

The first comment in **bold** is **THE NACISSIST SPEAKING**
The second comment is the **TRANSLATION**

I feel a sort of kinship with you.
YOU'RE A GREAT TARGET. I'M LINING YOU UP AS MY NEXT VICTIM. WONDER IF YOU'LL FALL FOR THE "YOU'RE MY SOULMATE" LINE?

I have finally met my match.
THIS LINE WORKS REALLY WELL SO I SAY IT TO EVERY ONE OF MY TARGETS... LET'S HOPE THEY NEVER MEET AND SHARE NOTES!

I see something in you.
I CAN EXPLOIT, USE AND ABUSE YOU FOR MY OWN NEEDS. YOU HAVE A LOT TO OFFER!

I need to hear your voice.
I NEED TO HEAR YOU TELL ME HOW PERFECT, WONDERFUL AND SMART I AM. I NEED YOU TO STROKE MY EGO.

I really need some intimacy with you.
SLEEP WITH ME NOW.

I value you.
YOU'RE GREAT NARCISSISTIC SUPPLY AND YOU MAKE ME LOOK REALLY GOOD TO OTHERS.

Maybe I am not the right person for you.
I AM GOING TO "SOW THE SEEDS OF DOUBT" IN YOU SO THAT YOU WILL WORK HARDER TO MAKE ME HAPPY AND PLEASE ME ME ME!

I'm just trying to take care of myself.
MYSELF BEING THE OPERATIVE WORD HERE BECAUSE I AM THE ONLY
ONE WHO MATTERS. WHY SHOULD I TAKE CARE OF MY RELATIONSHIP?
I AM SO WONDERFUL THAT I CAN FIND ANOTHER TARGET EASILY!

It's not all about you, you know...
RIGHT, BECAUSE IT'S ALL ABOUT ME ME ME ME ME!!!!!

**Have you always been like this? Has any other man told you
that?**
IF I MAKE YOU FEEL BAD ABOUT YOURSELF, YOU WILL FEAR BEING
ALONE AND WILL NEVER FIGURE OUT THAT I AM THE ONE WHO IS
DISTURBED, SICK AND INHUMAN.

**What's with the flannel pajamas? Why don't you want to look
good for me?**
I AM ONLY TURNED ON BY WHORES, STRIPPERS, PROSTITUTES AND
PORN. I HAVE A RAGING MADONNA-WHORE COMPLEX. BECAUSE YOU
ARE GOOD AND SWEET TO ME, YOU HAVE BECOME SEXLESS IN MY
EYES.

Who takes care of you better than I do?
I WANT YOU TO THINK YOU CAN'T TAKE CARE OF YOURSELF SO YOU
WILL BECOME DEPENDENT ON ME. I'M GOING TO TAKE OVER YOUR
LIFE, TURN YOU INTO MY PUPPET AND HAVE SOME FUN!

You took that out of context.
DAMN, YOU'RE ON TO ME. I NEED TO MAKE YOU THINK YOU'RE LOSING
YOUR MIND AND IMAGINING THINGS. I WILL DENY EVERYTHING I
SAID.

It's like walking on eggshells living with you... I never know

what mood you will be in next.
PROJECTION! TOTAL PROJECTION!!

If you really love me, you would understand me.
YOU NEED TO ANTICIPATE MY NEEDS BETTER! I EQUATE GETTING EXACTLY WHAT I WANT WITH SOMEONE'S LOVE.

Think of our children and what this is doing to them.
I'LL USE ANYTHING TO GUILT TRIP YOU AND HAVE NO SHAME USING OUR CHILDREN AS PAWNS.

I think I'm a really good person for you to know.
I'M GOING TO SUCK YOU DRY AND TAKE YOU FOR ALL YOU'RE WORTH!

No one knows you better than I do.
NO ONE WILL EVER UNDERSTAND YOU OR TOLERATE YOU THE WAY I DO.

I will never change.
I DON'T SEE ANY REASON TO CHANGE. I'M PERFECT.

You need someone to tell you what to do.
I WANT YOU TO FEEL SO DEPENDENT AND INCOMPETENT YOU HAVE TO ASK MY PERMISSION TO BREATHE. I CONTROL YOUR REALITY AND YOUR LIFE!

I'll take care of it. I have to take care of everything.

I WANT YOU TO BELIEVE YOU CAN'T DO ANYTHING RIGHT. I AM NOT GOING TO ALLOW YOU TO HAVE AN INDEPENDENT THOUGHT BECAUSE I NEED TO KEEP YOU DEPENDENT ON ME.

You read too much into everything.
YOU'RE GETTING CLOSE TO FIGURING ME OUT. DAMN YOU!

You know that's not what I meant to say, so stop twisting my words
TWISTING WORDS IS MY THING!!!

I'm not going to get into this right now!
YOU'RE CATCHING ON TO ME... I AM GOING TO SHAME DUMP AND GUILT-TRIP YOU SO YOU WILL STOP QUESTIONING ME.

Why would you stay with someone who abuses you and come back for more?
IT'S ALL YOUR FAULT I'M ABUSING YOU.

You were abusive to me.
(PROJECTION) I WAS ABUSIVE TO YOU AND I DIDN'T LIKE YOU CALLING ME ON IT. I SHOULD BE ABLE TO TREAT YOU HOWEVER I WANT WITH NO CONSEQUENCES.

You were not appreciative of all I did for you.
AND NO MATTER WHAT YOU DID FOR ME, IT WOULD NEVER BE ENOUGH.

What's so hard about throwing your arms around me?
I DESERVE LOVE, AFFECTION AND ADORATION. WHY AREN'T YOU WORSHIPPING ME?!

Are you really as secure and confident as you portray to be?
I WANT YOU TO DOUBT YOURSELF SO YOU RELY ON ME COMPLETELY.

I did it to protect you.

74

I DID IT TO PROTECT ME BUT NOW I AM GOING TO MAKE YOU FEEL
BAD BY BACKWARD TALKING!

I didn't want to make you paranoid.
WHAT I REALLY DIDN'T WANT WAS FOR YOU TO FIND OUT! DAMN YOU!

You have commitment issues.
YOU WON'T IGNORE THE WAY I USE AND EXPLOIT YOU. YOU WANT A
REAL, HONEST, HUMAN RELATIONSHIP. I AM NOT HUMAN, BUT I'LL
TELL YOU THAT YOU'RE THE ONE WITH ISSUES.

You always think you're right and never back down.
YOU'RE GETTING WAY TOO SMART FOR ME - HOW I CAN MAKE YOU
DOUBT YOURSELF? OH YEAH...I KNOW...BLAME YOU FOR DEFENDING
YOURSELF!

Would i lie to you?
I ALWAYS LIE TO YOU, EVERYONE ELSE AND EVEN MYSELF.

Why couldn't you have just agreed to disagree?
WHY COULDN'T YOU HAVE LET ME WIN AND DO WHATEVER I WANT.

I left you because of the way you treated me.
I LEFT BECAUSE YOU STARTED TO FIGURE ME OUT.

We argued all the time.
YOU WOULDN'T LET ME WALK ALL OVER YOU!

Sex is a hassle, isn't it?
I'D RATHER TOSS OFF - I PREFER TO HAVE SEX WITH MYSELF.

I would love to be with you but I can't stand the underlying

anger.

I DON'T LIKE WHEN WOMEN HAVE A MIND OF THEIR OWN AND START TO SEE THROUGH ALL MY BULLSHIT. THE ONLY PERSON ENTITLED TO THEIR ANGER IS ME ME ME!!

You are just too difficult.

YOU ARE TOO SMART AND STARTING TO WAKE UP FROM THE MIND CONTROL.

Your expectations are unreasonable.

I CAN'T GIVE YOU WHAT YOU WANT BECAUSE I AM NOT HUMAN. LET'S MAKE THIS YOUR FAULT BY TELLING YOU THAT YOUR EXPECTATIONS ARE TOO HIGH.

Good luck finding someone who will put up with you.

I WANT YOUR SELF-ESTEEM TO BE NON-EXISTENT SO EVEN WHEN I'M GONE MY WORDS CONTROL YOUR MIND FOREVER!

Your character will never change.

HOW DARE YOU BE STRONG ENOUGH TO RIP OFF MY MASK!

You never loved me enough.

IT'S ALL ABOUT ME ME ME AND YOU STOPPED GIVING ME SUPPLY AND WORSHIPPING THE GROUND I WALK ON.

Talking to you is to fight with you.

I LOVE FIGHTING & DRAMA - I LIVE FOR IT! I CREATE CHAOS - IT MAKES ME FEEL POWERFUL!

Stop attacking me.

I DON'T LIKE BEING HELD ACCOUNTABLE FOR ANYTHING! HOW DARE YOU QUESTION ME AND RIP MY FALSE MASK OFF!

I fear we are going to have a big misunderstanding and never talk again.
I'M GOING TO CREATE A SITUATION THAT JUSTIFIES ME DISCARDING AND DEVALUING YOU AND MAKE YOU BELIEVE IT'S YOUR FAULT - IT WILL MAKE YOUR HEAD SPIN!

I will always love you.
I KNOW SAYING THAT "LOVE" WORD GETS ME WHAT I WANT. SO I'LL SAY IT EVEN THOUGH I AM CLUELESS AS TO WHAT IT REALLY MEANS.

We will always be attracted to each other.
I'LL PLANT THIS ONE IN YOUR BRAIN TO ENSURE I CAN COME AROUND AND SLEEP WITH YOU WHENEVER I WANT.

I see how happy you are and it's killing me.
I CAN'T STAND PEOPLE OTHER THAN ME BEING HAPPY! I GET OFF ON HURTING PEOPLE AND MANIPULATING THEIR EMOTIONS.

I guess this relationship has not been healthy for you.
WOW I FEEL SO GOOD INSIDE KNOWING HOW BAD I MESSED YOU UP. I AM SO POWERFUL! ME ME ME!!

I'm gonna see you again, we have mutual friends.
I AM GONNA STALK YOU AND FOLLOW YOU AND HARASS YOU SO BUCKLE UP, BABY!

Why are you being like this?
WHY ARE YOU ASKING ME TO BE HUMAN AND HAVE FEELINGS? I JUST

WANNA SLEEP WITH YOU. DANG YOUR NASTY BRAIN... YOU'RE GONNA RIP MY MASK OFF & REALIZE I AM USING YOU.

You drag me down.

YOU ARE TOO MUCH REALITY FOR ME... I AM SPECIAL AND YOU ARE NOT WORSHIPPING ME THE WAY I SHOULD BE WORSHIPPED RIGHT NOW SO I HAVE NO USE FOR YOU.

I need to be myself.

SO I AM OFF TO FIND SOME NEW PREY – I.E. A NEW WOMAN TO PUT UP WITH MY SELFISH NEEDS AND WORSHIP THE GROUND I WALK ON UNTIL I GET TIRED OF HER, THAT IS. I WILL ALWAYS TIRE OF MY SUPPLY AS I AM ADDICTED TO FINDING NEW SOURCES OF SUPPLY. NEW SUPPLY IS MY DRUG OF CHOICE!

I feel like I've ruined your life!

I KNOW I RUINED YOUR LIFE SO ADMIT IT TO ME SO I CAN FEEL POWERFUL AND OMNIPOTENT!

I never watch porn.

I NEVER WATCH PORN WHEN I THINK I AM GONNA GET CAUGHT, BUT I AM COMPLETELY ADDICTED TO IT. I EXPECT EVERY WOMAN I MEET TO LOOK, ACT AND PERFORM LIKE A PORN STAR. IF NOT, I HAVE NO USE FOR THEM.

We have to communicate better.

YOU ARE NO LONGER DOING WHAT I DEMAND YOU DO. I HAD YOU NICE & CONTROLLED - YOU NEED TO GO BACK TO BEING CONTROLLED!

I will always love you unconditionally.

I READ THIS IN A BOOK SOMEWHERE... MAYBE IT WILL WORK.

Selective Memory

As humans, we have what is called *Selective Memory*, which our mind uses as a way to protect us. Good memories are vividly clear and much more readily available for recall in our memory than bad memories. Bad memories are fragmented, stored in a different part of the brain and not as easily accessible.

Selective memory means that instead of remembering how horribly our partner treated us, our brains access good memories much more readily. We avoid bad memories, but positive memories are easily accessible at any time. This puts us at a significant disadvantage when trying to stay away from our narcissist. Instead of remembering all the bad things, we remember the good times and begin idealizing the relationship.

We must be mindful of this happening and the best way of doing this is to create a list of what we will not forget. For the next writing assignment, create a bullet point list of all the cruel things your narcissist did, which made you feel sad, angry, fearful or ashamed. We will call this the *What I Will Not Forget List.*

Every time you think of something hurtful your narcissist did or he does something new to hurt you, add it to the list. Doing this will help you resist him when he tries to win you back. By documenting this information, you create a silent weapon of defense to turn to when you need to remind yourself of why you should never be with him again.

A University of Michigan psychology researcher, Robin Edelstein, found that people who block out unpleasant memories may enjoy short-term gains but cause long-term consequences by emotionally detaching themselves. People who block out or avoid painful memories worry Edelstein the most. She explains:

"While avoiding things can be a helpful short-term strategy, not paying attention to certain things for extended periods of time might be bad for your mental health with consequences for your physical health. All the effort to avoid anxiety actually creates more anxiety later."

CHAPTER 4

STEP FOUR
GET REAL

We no longer deny reality and are ready to face our anger and fear.

This step is dedicated to dealing with the feelings that are the most difficult to process and confront. These feelings are anger and fear. We avoid these emotions like the plague. There are many reasons for this, but unfortunately few of us realize how avoiding these feelings keeps us stuck, just like the narcissist. It is critical to realize:

We must Get Real *to Heal!*

When you are in a state of fear and anger, what is missing?

LOVE – your most powerful emotional state – is missing. It all starts with yourself. We all know, no one can love you unless you love yourself first.

Do you recall when I explained the emotional capacity of a narcissist? I described them as being stuck living in anger and fear. They have not developed the more complex feelings that make us human, like love and compassion, because they have never learned how to fully process feelings of anger and fear.

In my opinion, anger and fear are our most powerful emotions. They are the most powerful because they are the most motivating of all feelings. Anger and fear can motivate you to make necessary changes in your life or they can paralyze you to remain stuck in a state of pain.

Anger

Let's look at anger first. Many of us were taught to repress anger, especially women. Anger has a negative connotation because most people associate it with aggression. But in reality, anger is followed by violence only 10 percent of the time, according to Howard Kassinove, PH.D., co-author of "Anger Management: The Compete Treatment Guide for Practice."

Many of us are conditioned to feel shame for feeling any feelings of anger. Anger runs deep. We may have feelings of anger towards members of our family, but we refuse to acknowledge these feelings. We're afraid if we acknowledge our anger about it, it will mean we do not love them. However, it is important to realize that this is irrational and keeps us stuck. We must feel our feelings to heal. It is ok to be angry about how we were treated in the past. We must acknowledge and honor our feelings. We are entitled to feel the way we do.

We may not only feel shame, but in the case of our narcissist, we simply do not want to face the truth. To face the truth means we have to make changes in our life that will not be easy. It takes courage to get real. I know I buried my head in the sand for years at the end of my marriage. I did not want to admit that my marriage was not working. It is simply easier to deny things sometimes. However, to deny our feelings is to deny our true self and is no way to live.

Used productively, anger can help us restore our self-esteem and exert more control over our lives. Processing our anger is absolutely critical to our recovery. However, we must be careful in how we process it. As we touched on earlier, anger is neither a positive or negative emotion. How we RESPOND and REACT to anger is what makes all the difference in the world. The key is not to avoid anger, the key is to learn how to RESPOND to anger.

"What happens is not as important as how you react to what happens." ~ Thaddeus Gola

The idea of constructive anger is gaining a great deal of empirical support lately. Research tells us that processing our anger in productive ways leads to health benefits. Experts say that constructive anger can improve intimate and work relationships.

It is one thing to stay silent when you disagree with someone or something, but quite another to simply allow others to walk all over you. Some of you may just be starting to realize what an abusive relationship you were really in. I would guarantee that feelings of anger and resentment towards your significant other are what finally caused you to see the light and take action. Anger is a natural defense mechanism designed to protect us from abuse. We should never deny our feelings of anger.

Anger like all feelings is a normal, healthy and essential emotion. Getting angry does not make you a bad person. Personally, I believe without this instinct we would be extinct. Anger is a biological safeguard to ensure our survival. Anger is our body's response to internal or external demands, threats and pressures. Anger warns us that there is a problem or a potential threat. At the same time, it gives us courage to face the problem or meet the threat by providing us with a release of the hormone adrenaline.

Adrenaline prepares us to meet the threat by raising our defenses and giving us a boost of energy. This in turn provides us with added strength to fight off our enemy or added speed in which to run from the enemy. Think of Darwin's survival of the fittest theory. We should never ignore our emotions. They exist for a reason: to warn us, protect us and guide us through life.

Cruel behavior or abusive remarks from others should not be tolerated. We have a right to be angry when someone hurts or insults us. It is a threat to our emotional well-being. Anger is the emotion that alerts us that something is wrong and causes us to finally take action.

Do not hide from your anger. You must recognize it as a signal that there is a problem that needs to be resolved. We become angry because there is an issue of some kind that requires our attention. In my opinion, anger is like an internal alarm system telling us something is wrong. To ignore it is dangerous.

Research tells us women who do not acknowledge anger or do not process anger in a healthy way are more vulnerable to health problems. Rates of diagnosed breast cancer are found to be higher in women who have never openly expressed their anger.

"Holding on to anger is like grasping a hot coal with the intent of throwing it at someone else; You are the one who gets burned."
~ Hindu Prince Gautama Siddharta

Do not repress your anger. Acknowledging your anger is the first step in releasing resentment and ultimately allows you to move on. Forgiveness is a personal choice each of us should make. Everyone's situation is different. I can't possibly make a blanket statement about whether one should forgive their abuser without knowing the circumstances.

On the other hand, I do think it is critical we forgive ourselves for falling for someone who wasn't who we thought they were. We must not beat ourselves up for the time we spent in a toxic relationship. We did absolutely nothing wrong but believe in the goodness of another human being. Forgiving ourselves is essential.

Hopefully, you're beginning to see the importance of acknowledging and processing your feelings of anger when they occur. If we do not allow ourselves to feel anger, we lose out on the benefits of it – motivation, strength, energy, power and protection.

Many of us do not realize just how powerful a force anger can be. When anger is used to motivate us to make life changes that promote our emotional well-being, it is positive. However, when we express anger through aggressive or passive-aggressive means, it is negative.

Anger can motivate you to make needed changes in your life or it can make you emotionally and physically ill if you hold it in. It can empower you or it can kill your relationships if you take your anger out on someone in the wrong way. Instead of being honest and acknowledging their anger, many people shift blame, project and abuse others.

"It's not the load that breaks you down, it's the way you carry it." ~ Lena Horne

I believe the way you handle your anger affects all of your relationships, including your relationship with yourself. Many of us are so afraid of anger that we direct the anger inward at ourselves instead of expressing it outward. Others take their anger out on innocent people. Anger externalized can lead to violence, while anger internalized causes depression and health problems.

Why is it that we feel there are only two responses to anger – to blame others or blame ourselves? Why does someone always have to be right and someone else have to be wrong? Thinking in black and white terms like this closes us down and makes our world smaller. Wanting things to fit in a perfect little box is futile. We will only find ourselves banging our head against the wall in frustration instead of learning from the experience. If we allow ourselves to learn from the disagreement, we may realize there are much needed changes we need to make in our life.

If your narcissist cheated on you, you may try to blame the person he had an affair with and focus your anger there. However, it is important to recognize that by blaming someone else, you are denying the truth about the reality of your situation. Instead of dealing with the fact that the person you love cheated on you, you are wasting time being mad at someone else.

This just keeps us stuck and will only slow down our recovery process. Until we can acknowledge who we are really angry at, we will never work through our feelings so we can move on. At the end of the day, we must look at our relationship, deal with the reality of it and get honest with ourselves in order to move on.

As you know, I believe life is all about how we RESPOND to it. We need to open our minds and heart to stay in the uncertainty where we don't need to define who is right or who is wrong in every situation. It doesn't matter. What matters is what you learn from it. What is your experience? This is living. This is open space. Everything is ambiguous and always changing, shifting. Finding absolute right and wrong is a trick we play on ourselves to think we're in control. We think it helps us feel safe and secure.

Unfortunately, it does the opposite. It makes us more uneasy because we know we're lying to ourselves. Subconsciously, we know this. Instead of lying or hiding from the truth, we must be compassionate with ourselves. We tell ourselves we want unconditional love from another person, yet we can't even give it to ourselves. Instead of acknowledging when we are wrong or when we have faults, we lie to ourselves that we are perfect. No one is perfect. To be with someone who unconditionally loves you means they accept you for who you are –

they take the good with the bad and they love you unconditionally.

Why can't we do this for ourselves?!

Until we can do this for ourselves, we will never live an authentic life. We must be honest and compassionate with ourselves. This is referred to as *loving-kindness* in Buddhism. We must go easy on ourselves to find love for the parts of ourselves that aren't perfect. We must have an unconditional relationship with ourselves. If we can't love ourselves, we cannot expect anyone else to love us.

You will remain in a state of pain, darkness or unhappiness as long as you continue to lie to yourself and deny your reality. You must have a total commitment to reality in order to heal. The more you resist the present moment, the more pain you create within yourself.

We must get to know the nature of our restlessness and fear. It is how we get to know ourselves on the deepest level possible. To live an authentic life, we must *get real to heal*. Many people are afraid of the truth. However, to finally confront the truth is the most liberating and freeing thing you can do for yourself. It is truly transformative.

Fear

Let's talk about fear now. What prevents us from looking honestly at our situation?

FEAR

Whatever we fear controls us. Fear, if not confronted, prevents us from truly living. Fear is like a prison.

"The only thing we have to fear is fear itself." ~ *Franklin D. Roosevelt*

Powerful words, right? Well, fear is a very powerful emotion. We live in a society that throws fear in our face at every opportunity. Marketers sell to us by playing on our fear. The government uses fear to control us and keep us complacent. Society encourages us to distract ourselves from fear by numbing ourselves with alcohol, drugs or pills. We are so afraid of fear that it paralyzes us.

As mentioned earlier, our modern culture has conditioned us to avoid pain and seek pleasure and to think only in terms of dualities or complete opposites. Instead of finding a balance, we are led to believe that everything has to be either:

RIGHT OR WRONG

BLACK OR WHITE

FAIR OR UNFAIR

CERTAIN OR UNCERTAIN

….and here's the biggest misconception that ruins our entire view of life:

PLEASURE OR PAIN

Yes, we are conditioned and programmed to think we can:

SEEK PLEASURE AND AVOID PAIN

Everything we do is centered around running from pain and enhancing pleasure. But guess what? Guess what is so fundamentally wrong with this?

And this lesson (besides learning to live in the moment) has changed my life and my attitude towards everything...

We cannot avoid pain. To think we can is ignorant. Yet, many of us spend our lives fooling ourselves to think we can. Suffering is part of the human condition. It is part of life. We lie to ourselves that everything is ok when it's not. It is this behavior that keeps us stuck and dead inside.

"Pain and pleasure, like light and darkness, succeed each other."
~ Laurence Stern

We must accept that with pleasure comes pain and with pain comes pleasure. We must learn to live in the grey and stop trying to force certainty in life where there can be none. The more we deny our reality and lie to ourselves, the deeper we put ourselves in the dark.

Unfortunately, this is how many of us learned how to get through the tough times. We have learned to use denial as a coping mechanism. What we fail to realize is that the very method we thought was helping us is really killing us inside.

"God instructs the heart not by ideas, but by pains and contradictions." ~ Jean Pierre De Caussade

When something hurts in life, we typically avoid it. We rarely think of it as something we are meant to learn from. In fact, we immediately try to find a way to get rid of the painful feeling and tell ourselves we will be happy when something else we've been waiting for happens. For example, we tell ourselves when we move into our new home we'll be happy, or when we meet our soul mate, we will be happy. I lived this way for years, telling myself I'll be happy when such and such happens. We could spend the rest of our lives telling ourselves this. It is no way to go through life. It is a vicious cycle that never ends.

We run away thinking we can avoid our reality, but what we don't realize is:

Nothing ever goes away until it has taught us what we need to know.

We can lie to ourselves or run all we want, but the lesson will keep returning in different forms and manifestations until we learn what it is trying to teach us about our reality. The very first noble truth the Buddha points out is that suffering is inevitable in human beings. It is part of the human condition. We cannot avoid it.

We must accept suffering and open our hearts to look at how weak we are being by trying to avoid it. Only then can we discover that the very thing that terrifies us is in fact a way for us to reconnect with our true self. Facing reality shows you who you are and what is true. Facing our fear and waking up tells us something about ourselves. We must get to know fear, become familiar and intimate with it. It teaches us something. When we stop running and don't act out, repress or blame, we encounter our true self.

Fear

Who am I

Who will I become

Can I make a difference

Or will I ever overcome

This fear I have

What is this fear

I can feel it near

But I can't quite hear

What awaits me

What lies ahead

Am I too afraid

Of a world of dread

I must fight my fear

For it's the only way

To live a life of

Excitement every day

I wrote this poem as I was graduating college. I know, kind of hokey, but I just recently found it in one of my journals and it made me think. At the time I wrote it, I remember trying desperately to figure out what this fear was that was holding me back. I couldn't pinpoint what it was exactly, but it was overwhelming.

It has taken some time, but today I recognize what that fear is.....

FEAR OF THE UNKNOWN....UNCERTAINTY

We do not like uncertainty in life. In fact, we dread it. Yet, nothing in life is certain. This is another truth we must accept. I spent years of my life trying to force certainty where there could be none, and it only led to obsessive thought that distracted me from the present moment. We cannot force anything in life. It is a losing battle. My therapist always told me I must "learn to live in the grey" and this has helped me tremendously.

Life is messy. We have to stop thinking in extremes - black and white thinking is not healthy. Things do not have to be all good or all bad. They can be somewhere in the middle, and to be honest, that's really what we should expect. We should never expect perfection.

Life is a journey...an adventure. We must celebrate this and not be afraid of it. Learning to live in the grey means we accept uncertainty in life. It wasn't until I accepted that we're not supposed to know what's going to happen next in life that I finally started to thrive and truly live.

Acceptance

We often upset ourselves as a result of how we choose to RESPOND to life. Most disturbance comes from the belief that we should be able to control others in an attempt to control ourselves. Unfortunately, what we fail to realize is the only person we can control is ourselves.

Instead of focusing on what we cannot change or control, we must focus our efforts on that which we can control. The Serenity Prayer is a wonderful reminder of this:

The Serenity Prayer

Grant me the...

Serenity to accept the things I cannot change,

Courage to change the things I can, and the

Wisdom to know the difference.

It is how we RESPOND to life that matters. Therefore, it is critical that we understand what we can and cannot control. We have choices in life, and while we cannot control what happens to us, we can control how we RESPOND to it. It is the choices we make after a setback that determine our destiny. My very wise older brother once told me:

"My proudest moments in life are not my achievements, but my ability to bounce off the lows in life; it's the climb and journey from that low that is most rewarding."

Acceptance is critical to begin the climb. In my opinion, until we accept our situation for what it is and all its ugliness and craziness, we will never move on. We must distinguish what we can control from what we cannot control. This is very important because it really helps us understand what is within our grasp and what is not. There is no point wasting energy on something we have absolutely no ability to control.

Doing this only makes us feel helpless and that is not the case. We have

94

an amazing ability to control our life if we focus on what we can control vs. what we cannot.

Everything outside of our control is something we must let go of so we can put all of our energy into the areas we can control. Identifying the difference between what we can control and what we cannot is absolutely essential. It helps us succeed in life and stay focused.

To illustrate this, please create two lists in your *Recovery Journal*. One list should include everything in your life that you can control while the other should include everything in your life that is outside of your control. Be sure you are honest with yourself.

Once this is done, go back and look at your two lists. Highlight the things you can control and cross out the things you cannot control. Do not waste your energy on the things you cannot control. You must let go of these things and only focus on what you can control.

The trick is to keep exploring and not bail out, even when we learn something we don't want to accept. Nothing is what we thought. Accepting truth puts you on the spot. At times, accepting truth may cause us to initially suffer. However, this is where we have a choice. We must realize we are on the verge of something. We can choose to shut down and feel resentful, or we can hone in on the throbbing quality of truth. It is a testing of sorts...a testing of our ability to awaken our hearts.

When things feel like they can't get any worse, we have a choice. We may think the point is to pass the test or overcome the problem, but the truth is that some things cannot be solved. They must be accepted. Things come together and fall apart all the time.

The healing comes from allowing these things to happen. Much obsessing comes from trying to control the unknown. Until we accept the fact that we cannot control the unknown, a constant battle will ensue in our minds. The reason for this is because deep down, we know we cannot control everything. To fool ourselves into thinking we can only adds to our *Cognitive Dissonance*.

We may think something is going to bring us pleasure, but it does not. We may think something is going to bring us misery, but it may not. The truth is, we don't know. We must learn to accept the fact that we don't know what's really going to happen. Allowing ourselves to realize we don't know what is going to happen is the most healing lesson of all. After all, life is a journey. As long as we stay mindful and are honest with ourselves, we have the strength to face what life may bring us.

To avoid pain and seek pleasure will only lead to unhappiness. In order to think we can avoid suffering, we must lie to ourselves about our reality. We either lie to ourselves about our reality or we completely escape from it altogether. Either way, we are not living authentically. We must experience each moment to its fullest.

Running away is like preferring death to life. We may be in the dark right now, but from darkness comes light. If we commit ourselves to feeling our emotions and staying right where we are, our experience becomes vivid. Things become very clear when we don't try to escape or run from them.

"One's action ought to come out of an achieved stillness: not to be mere rushing on." ~ *D.H. Lawrence*

One's ability to remain still is a sign that they are in touch with themselves and live a life with their eyes wide open. They do not hide from reality or run, but instead face it head on. To achieve inner stillness is a skill we should all develop.

We must get to know fear and become familiar with fear. Look it right in the eye. In my opinion, it is the only way to undo negative patterns of thinking. If we face something head on, we no longer play mind games with ourselves to avoid it.

When we face fear, we will be humbled. There will be little room for the arrogance of holding onto ideals or lying to ourselves as a method of escaping reality.

The kinds of discoveries that are made in painful situations have much to do with having the courage to feel. When we stop and feel our feelings, we encounter our true being. We are more in touch with ourselves than ever before. This is what Buddhists call *Mindfulness*. Clarity provides direction. We must never fear the reality of our situation, no matter how overwhelming it may seem.

"Ruin is a gift. Ruin is the road to transformation."
~ Elizabeth Gilbert

CHAPTER 5

STEP FIVE
WAKE UP

We tap into the power of our mind to awaken our spirit and find ourselves again.

Whatever arises, we must not judge. We must not avoid. We must use everything that happens to us as a means for waking up. We must reverse our habitual pattern of trying to avoid pain by allowing ourselves to feel the moment and understand what it is we are meant to learn from it. We must stop looking for alternatives and cheat ourselves of the present moment.

Unlike the narcissist, engaging the ego is an OPTION for us. We must remember to let go of our ego and discipline ourselves not to escape reality. Instead, we must practice acceptance. The ego always feels threatened and always lives in a state of fear and want. Once you understand this, you must step out of it so you can:

Get Real, Wake Up and Heal!

Face your fear. Surrender your ego! When we do not run, we discover our innermost essence. Whatever arises, we do not judge. Give up the idea that pain can be avoided and have the courage to relax with the reality of your situation.

Do not avoid your personal experience thinking there is something better out there. We must totally commit to our reality. Only then do we experience the world fully. We must stop thinking we can just run away. Only when we don't hold back and prepare to escape, do we experience life and truly find ourselves. Commit to staying in the moment. Things become very clear when there is nowhere to escape.

"We can easily forgive a child who is afraid of the dark: the real tragedy of life is when men are afraid of the light." ~ Plato

To accept uncertainty and stay with it is the path to true awakening. Sticking with uncertainty and learning not to panic or run is the path to spirituality. Accepting that we cannot control everything and everyone around us is to let go of our ego. Being pre-occupied with our self-image, what others think of our success and failure is like being deaf and blind. We lose sight of what is important and that is our relationship with ourselves.

Embrace the moment and be open to what you are supposed to learn from it. Wake up and allow yourself to experience pain. It is a fundamental part of life. We think by protecting ourselves from suffering we are being kind to ourselves. This could not be further from the truth. In fact, by doing this we are only becoming more fearful. This alienates us and hardens us. We disconnect from ourselves without even realizing it. If we shield ourselves from discomfort, we will suffer.

Many people never let their guard down to love another person because they are so afraid of getting hurt. Those who live with a guarded heart are not living. They are merely existing and their existence is a sad one.

"It is better to have loved and lost than never to have loved at all." ~ Alfred Lord Tennyson

We must wake up and let go of our ego. We must find a balance between thinking everything has to be defined as either all good or all bad. As we discussed earlier, black and white thinking is toxic. We must learn to live in the grey. Acknowledging that life is messy and never perfect is the first step to waking up and living in the moment. It allows us to discover our innermost essence. We must learn how to allow ourselves to stay in the moment and connect with the richness of it, the rawness of it, the tenderness of it and the pain of it.

"All the world is full of suffering. It is also full of overcoming." ~
Hellen Keller

When we don't close off and let our hearts break, we not only find ourselves, but we discover our kinship with all beings. This is why our on-line forum is so powerful. Connecting with others on a level no one else can and in a manner that is so raw and real is life-changing. Together, we help each other face the truth. Yes, it can be excruciatingly painful but at the same time, is absolutely essential in order to heal and move on. To me, this is the essence of waking up. *Bochichista* is a Buddhist term for a noble or awakened heart and describes this process beautifully.

To try to avoid pain and suffering is to live a false existence. It is a lie to tell yourself you can avoid pain. To fend off how we feel only hardens us. We should not be afraid to feel. We should not be ashamed of the love and grief it invokes in us. I would rather feel pain and know I'm alive than feel nothing. We must take it all in. Let the pain of the world touch your heart and turn it into compassion for yourself and others.

It is a process. Learning not to run away or lie to ourselves about our reality takes time. Running away is so deep-seated in us. We are conditioned so that the minute things get tough or we even think things are going to get tough, we run. The trick is to avoid running and commit to the moment....to stay there and deal with it. Instead of manipulating the situation or lying to ourselves, we allow ourselves to be with it and understand what we are meant to learn from it. It starts by learning to love ourselves unconditionally.

Let It Be
Songwriters: John Lennon & Paul McCartney

When I find myself in times of trouble
Mother Mary comes to me
Speaking words of wisdom, let it be

And in my hour of darkness
She is standing right in front of me
Speaking words of wisdom, let it be

Let it be, let it be
Let it be, let it be
Whisper words of wisdom
Let it be

And when the brokenhearted people
Living in the world agree
There will be an answer, let it be

For though they may be parted
There is still a chance that they will see
There will be an answer, let it be

Let it be, let it be
Let it be, let it be
Yeah, there will be an answer let it be

Let it be, let it be
Let it be, let it be
Whisper words of wisdom
Let it be

Let it be, let it be
Let it be, yeah, let it be

Whisper words of wisdom
Let it be

And when the night is cloudy
There is still a light that shines on me
Shine on until tomorrow, let it be

I wake up to the sound of music
Mother Mary comes to me
Speaking words of wisdom, let it be

Yeah, let it be, let it be
Let it be, yeah, let it be
There will be an answer, let it be

Let it be, let it be
Let it be, yeah, let it be
Whisper words of wisdom
Let it be

Find Your Spirituality

I am a spiritual person, but not a religious person. The beauty of nature and miracle of life prove to me that a higher power exists beyond myself. I believe this higher power exists everywhere. We do not need to go to a church or a temple to be close to God. If that is something that helps us feel closer, then it's a wonderful thing to do. However, I know that in order to be close to God, I do not need to be anywhere other than with myself. God is within each one of us. It is this realization that has allowed me to find my spirituality.

The kingdom of heaven is within you. (Luke 17:21)

I believe getting in touch with your spirituality has nothing to do with where you pray or to what religion you conform. Instead, it has everything to do with tapping into the spiritual potential that exists within you.

Jesus was not a magician or a performer. He was a teacher. He taught us that any person who makes the discovery of the God-like potential within him has the innate potential to be transformed by the power of their own divinity.

Jesus taught us that God exists within each one of us. He discovered his own divinity and sought to teach us how to tap into ours by getting in touch with our true consciousness. When he says "Follow Me," he is asking us to reach within ourselves to find the high level of consciousness that he achieved. For it is in this level of being that we are truly alive. I see Jesus as the great discoverer of the divinity of humankind. He does not want to be worshipped. He wants to be followed as a teacher for helping us find ourselves and our true level of consciousness.

Ye shall know the truth and the truth shall make you free.
(John 8:32)

In my opinion, this freedom is the inward motivation to tap into the raw spiritual power that resides within us. It is to harness our true potential and move in the direction of our divine good. In a way, it is like turning on a light within ourselves where we become conscious of the root of our true being and consciously make the decision to tap into our spirituality. By finding it, we are more creative, imaginative, powerful and great.

All of us are spiritual beings, whether we know it or not, whether we act on it or not. Unfortunately, in today's world, we are more in touch with

105

our physical being than our spiritual being. We must remember that our physical being is only a shell that holds our spiritual being and this shell is only temporary. It is our spiritual being, our soul, which never dies. We must tap into our God-like potential, that light that resides within each one of us, to live a life that fosters good, helps others and has purpose.

When we are in touch with our spiritual self, we are free to do unlimited things. We see things in a different light, we tap into a creativity within ourselves we never knew existed and we draw upon a higher potential. This potential has always been within us, but it is our responsibility to find it and harness it. This is what Jesus taught us.

"For an impenetrable shield, stand inside yourself."
~ Ralph Waldo Emerson

I do not believe God intended for us to fight wars and kill each other over religion. Getting caught up in this causes us to miss the whole point of his message. He sent Jesus to teach us that it is not about how we worship him, but instead about reaching deep within ourselves to find the presence of God dwelling inside us. God is within each one of us and it is up to us to tap into the power and force of his spirit. I believe the moment we understand this, a whole new level of consciousness opens up that can change our lives forever.

God is really the essence of our being...our depth. Many of us try to define the undefinable, but perhaps it's easiest to think of God in terms of the depth of our being, our innate goodness and our divine potential.

We are all better than we realize. We have higher thoughts that we have yet to recognize.

You do not need to look "out there" to find your spirituality. It exists within you and always has. You can never be separated from God because you are an expression of God. God is within each one of us, waiting for us to harness his power. When we WAKE UP and allow ourselves to experience our true depth, we begin to truly live.

The Power of Your Mind

The human brain is amazingly powerful. Yet, until recently, we did not know how to harness its power. Thanks to recent advances in science and technology, we now know that our brains are much more plastic (changeable) than we ever thought. The concept of brain plasticity, known as Neuroplasticity, is one of the greatest scientific breakthroughs in the last decade. This field of research has proven that our brain is not permanently hardwired, but rather able to change physically, chemically and anatomically in response to our thoughts, experience and behavior. [1]

This means that we can alter and heal our brain by directing how we respond to stimuli. It is a step-by-step process and takes time, but we now know we can reverse the damage caused by emotional abuse and psychological trauma. As Dr. Frank Lawlis, author of "Retraining the Brain" states: "This is possibly as great a leap forward in public health as the discovery of antibiotics and vaccines."

When coming out of a relationship with a narcissist, it is important to remember that our minds are experiencing severe *Cognitive Dissonance*. As we now know, *Cognitive Dissonance* leads to obsessive, intrusive thoughts that impede our ability to concentrate, work, sleep, eat or function. It can often feel like we are in a fog or haze of some kind.

Our mind is not functioning properly because we have experienced psychological trauma and been the victim of brainwashing techniques.

107

Your narcissist used several different methods of coercion in order to control you. As discussed earlier, he threatened, degraded, shifted blame, criticized, manipulated, verbally assaulted, dominated, blackmailed, withdrew, withheld love and affection and *gaslighted* in an effort to make you feel as though you were going crazy.

He denied that events ever occurred or certain things were said. As a result, you doubt what you're hearing and seeing to the point that you begin to question your sanity. This is exactly what the narcissist set out to do. He wants you to believe you are imagining things and have some kind of mental illness or faulty memory.

When we doubt our perception of reality, the narcissist is able to control us knowing we are completely dependent on him for the truth. A narcissist wants us to believe we have problems and issues only he can understand and is willing to tolerate. By doing this, we start to feel unlovable, paranoid and doubtful, which ensures our dependence on him and his subsequent ability to control us. *Stockholm Syndrome* is a perfect example of how powerful this brainwashing can be.

It is critical we understand how we are being brainwashed and realize the only reason we feel addicted to them is because they have managed to create a false dependence within us. We must acknowledge this no matter how hard it is to accept. We have experienced emotional abuse and psychological trauma at the hands of the person we love. We have been brainwashed. The good news, however, is that we can deprogram and retrain our brain.

We now know it is possible to teach the brain to react in certain ways in situations in the same manner as it is possible to teach the body to move in new ways through physical therapy. I believe this information is all we need to know in order to rest assured that we will heal from these toxic relationships. It requires effort and certainly does not happen overnight, but trust me when I tell you that you can retrain your brain so you can disconnect from the powerful hold your narcissist has over you.

Until recently, we did not realize the incredible ability we have to retrain our brain. It makes sense if you think about it though. Look how easily the narcissist was able to brainwash you without you even knowing it. He used a very subtle and covert approach at first, yet was able to manipulate you to become completely dependent on him for survival. While you must accept that this has happened, the beautiful thing is that it is never too late to reverse the damage. It is now your turn to wake up, take back control of your life and retrain your brain!

Take Back Control

The key for my recovery has been the realization that while I cannot always control what happens to me in life, I can control how I RESPOND to it. Harnessing the power I have to retrain my brain and deprogram from a toxic relationship is what finally allowed me to heal and move on. I want to help you realize the same potential within yourself.

"It's not the strongest of the species that survives, nor the most intelligent, but the one most responsive to change."
~ Charles Darwin

Our society is undergoing a revolution in mental health with the newfound knowledge that we can retrain our brain. There are several methods on how to achieve this. Working with a Cognitive Behavioral

Therapist (CBT) to retrain my brain is what finally helped me move on. In my opinion, Cognitive Behavioral Therapy (CBT) is the most effective form of treatment for retraining your brain.

Cognitive Behavioral Therapy (CBT) is a type of treatment that has been around for the last forty to fifty years, but has just recently been gaining popularity. I believe it is easiest to begin explaining CBT by quoting Einstein's definition of insanity:

"Insanity is doing the same thing over and over, but expecting a different result." ~ Albert Einstein

We all are guilty of this at times. It is human nature. However, when it becomes a destructive pattern of behavior or negative thinking pattern, we must find a way to address it, right? Well, in my opinion, CBT is exactly what is required in order to change this kind of compulsive behavior.

Exposure Response Prevention (ERP) is the most common treatment in CBT and what it does is retrain your brain to respond differently to stimuli so you can stop engaging in self-destructive behavior. The idea being that responding differently will bring about a more positive result.

Cognitive therapy teaches us not to give others the power to upset us. We can easily allow other people or events to de-rail us and cause us great unhappiness. However, remember, it is not about what happens to us but how we RESPOND to it that matters, right?

CBT is a "doing" therapy whereby the licensed therapist takes you through different mental exercises in an effort to help retrain your brain. This therapy is not easy as the exercises can be difficult and anxiety provoking at times, but it is incredibly effective.

CBT is based on the belief that emotional disturbance is caused by distorted or irrational reasoning. Humans can be influenced to think illogically. This warped way of thinking can be acquired at any point in someone's life.

Obviously, as a result of the abusive relationship we were in, we were influenced to think illogically and doubt ourselves. We no longer trust our judgment and are experiencing severe anxiety. We have been brainwashed by our narcissist and need to deprogram from him. In my opinion, Cognitive Behavioral Therapy (CBT) is the most effective form of treatment for retraining your brain.

I do not suggest anyone endure the pain of recovering from a narcissist alone. I encourage you to seek professional help and attend support group meetings in your area if available. Our on-line forum is intended to assist you in your recovery, but certainly not meant to replace real therapy from a licensed mental health professional.

Whether you seek out treatment from a licensed mental health professional or certified life coach, there are certain fundamental aspects of retraining your brain that anyone can apply to their recovery program at any time. I'd like to share those with you now.

Retrain Your Brain

The most important thing to recognize when retraining your brain is that you are currently in a state of major anxiety. It is this anxiety that causes you to remain stuck and unable to focus on anything productive. You must acknowledge that you no longer want to remain in this negative pattern of thinking and will consciously make an effort to break free from it.

Webster defines anxiety as: "an abnormal and overwhelming sense of apprehension and fear often marked by physiological signs (as **sweating**, tension, and increased pulse), by doubt concerning the reality and nature of the threat, and by self-doubt about one's capacity to cope with it."

The key to retraining your brain is the ability to learn how to manage and cope with anxiety. It all comes down again to:

HOW YOU RESPOND

How you RESPOND to anxiety determines your ability to manage it. Everyone experiences anxiety. It is part of the human condition. 70 percent of adults report experiencing it daily and 30 percent report their anxiety levels are constant.[3]

"Things don't change. You change your way of looking at it, that's all." ~ Carlos Casteneda

Unfortunately, we are currently in a heightened state of constant anxiety as a result of the emotional abuse we experienced in a toxic relationship. We need to focus on retraining our brain. Heightened and prolonged anxiety can lead to obsessive-compulsive disorder, post-traumatic stress disorder, panic attacks and other phobias.

The key to retraining our brain is to: DESENSITIZE OURSELVES by controlling HOW WE RESPOND to anxiety in our lives.

"We are born into this world unarmed – our mind is our only weapon." ~ Ayn Rand

Manage Obsessive Thoughts

Here is what is happening in your mind when you experience anxiety:

Fear and stress trigger anxiety, which create noise and chaos that your brain cannot resolve. It is this noise that keeps you stuck and spinning in obsessive thought.

The key to stop obsessing is to prevent yourself from responding to the thoughts that cause you to obsess in the first place. You see, obsessive thoughts are a direct result of anxiety. Compulsions are what we do to try to reduce the anxiety....hence...obsessive-compulsive behavior.

Unfortunately, we think engaging in a compulsive behavior will lessen the anxiety, and it might initially, but it is only temporary. In fact, responding only increases the anxiety in the long run. Why? Because responding to the anxiety or obsessive thought in any way, shape or form only intensifies it. It validates it. We must not validate the thoughts.

You can observe the thoughts, but do not judge. Do not try to wish the thoughts away either because it will only cause you to think of them more. Do not fight your thoughts. To do so only creates more obsessive thought. Allow your thoughts to happen, but do not validate or judge them in any way. Laugh at the thoughts, dismiss them, but do not fight them off. Instead, simply observe, but do not judge or respond to them. To ignore them decreases their power.

Please allow me to forewarn you that I am going to be purposively redundant in this upcoming section, but understand I simply want to be sure you realize the incredible power you have to manage your thoughts.

The key is not to control WHAT you think (that is impossible).

The key is to control how you RESPOND to what you think.

The key to managing all anxiety is learning how to RESPOND to it.

For example, we have an anxiety provoking thought….

We have a CHOICE in how we RESPOND to it…

We judge and analyze the thought, thereby giving it significance, causing our mind to obsess and get stuck there…

Or

We do not judge or analyze the thought, thereby desensitizing ourselves to it and allowing our mind to move on…..

It is all in how we RESPOND

OBSESSIVE THOUGHT OR ANXIETY OCCURS….

RESPOND BY OBSERVING IT AND NOT JUDGING IT

= RELEASE IT & MOVE ON

OBSESSIVE THOUGHT OR ANXIETY OCCURS….

RESPOND BY JUDGING IT AND ANALYZING IT

= OBSESS MORE & GET STUCK

By controlling how we respond to our anxiety, we control our ability to manage it. For example, if we respond impulsively by trying to numb the anxiety or avoid it, we only increase the power and hold the thought has over us. However, if we respond with no judgment, we slowly desensitize ourselves to the fear, thereby lessening the control it has over us.

Simply observe the thought and realize that thoughts do not define you and are not a part of you. They are simply thoughts. Look at the obsessive thoughts as a separate entity and you will be able to distance yourself from them. The thoughts will always come. We have no control over that. Do not fight that. If you fight that, you're only setting yourself up for failure. It's like telling people not to look at the "elephant" in the room. Everyone is going to look, right?

Do not fight the thoughts or tell yourself not to think of them. Instead, you simply control how you RESPOND to the thoughts when they occur......because trust me, they will occur. You cannot prevent yourself from thinking thoughts. You can only control how you RESPOND to your thoughts. In my opinion, that is the fundamental key to successfully managing anxiety.

Everyone gets unwanted, intrusive thoughts. Yes, everyone. However, those who have not been brainwashed or emotionally abused do not over-analyze or judge these thoughts the way we do. They let random thoughts roll-off of them. They may just laugh and say, "Ha, what a strange thought" and then move on.

Unfortunately, this has become difficult for us to do because we are experiencing *Cognitive Dissonance* and possibly PTSD. As a result, we over-analyze and obsess about every little thought that pops into our mind. As I've said before, this is precisely what the narcissist counts on. If we feel paralyzed to act, confused by our thoughts and doubtful, we will never leave him. This is where he wants us... under his control... asking him to clarify what is truth and what is reality.

I am often asked by readers if obsessing about their narcissist means they belong together. Absolutely not! Thoughts of your narcissist do not mean you still love him, need him or should be with him. Thoughts of your narcissist simply mean he has managed to manipulate you to obsess over him and should be further proof that you need to deprogram from him.

Please know it means NOTHING that you are still thinking about your narcissist. It is not a sign that you should be with him. Like I said, the only thing it means is that he did an exceptional job of brainwashing you.

You must accept that you will have thoughts in the future about your narcissist that you would rather not have. They were a significant part of your life. It is natural to still think about him. In fact, it would be unnatural if you never thought of him.

You cannot control thoughts that come to mind. Memory is memory. Once created, it cannot be erased. However, the good news is you can control how you will RESPOND to the thoughts that pop into your head and that is the key to reducing your anxiety.

You must not fight off thoughts of your narcissist because they are going to arise. The key is not to judge the thoughts or respond to the thoughts when they do arise.

If you respond to the thoughts in any other way but indifference, you give them power and start the cycle of obsessive ideation.

So the key is not to fight the thoughts. Simply observe the thoughts. It is how you RESPOND to the thoughts that matter.

Try not to even think of them as your own thoughts but simply "intrusive thoughts" that prevent you from getting in touch with yourself. Looking at them in this way is helpful because the less you identify with the thoughts, the more quickly you can get back to your real self. The obsessive thoughts are just trying to distract you from feeling what you need to feel and doing what you need to do.

We can take back control. We can deprogram and begin to trust ourselves again. The key is not to judge your thoughts or give them any weight. The minute you judge a thought, you give it more power. The important thing to remember is a thought is a thought. That is it. You need not over-analyze it or judge it.

A member of our on-line forum put it very well when she said:

"It's ok to revisit places we have been in our lives (in our minds) but just don't throw out the anchor and stay there."

And you know what the anchor is? You know what causes you to get stuck?

When you:

JUDGE OR ANALYZE the thoughts.

The MOMENT you judge or analyze your thoughts is the MOMENT you.....

ANCHOR THEM & GET STUCK.

The longer you hold the anxiety, the heavier it will feel.

Thoughts are random. They don't define us. We cannot control them. They don't mean anything. There is no hidden or deeper meaning behind crazy thoughts or memories. In fact, some thoughts may even frighten you, but they are nothing more than white noise trying to distract you from having a REAL RELATIONSHIP with YOURSELF.

We will always have intrusive, unwanted thoughts. Everyone does. The good news is that we have a choice in how we want to RESPOND to these thoughts. Remember, life is not about what happens to us, it is about how we RESPOND to what happens to us.

Practicing this has helped me tremendously. I finally have peace of mind I never thought was possible. The thoughts still come, but by choosing how I will respond to these thoughts, I have reduced the power and the hold they have over me. I prevent myself from responding to the thoughts in any way that will intensify their strength.

They are only thoughts after all. Thoughts cannot hurt me, but how I RESPOND to my thoughts can hurt me. Being paralyzed with anxiety over thoughts is no way to live life. It prohibits us from truly living and experiencing all life has to offer.

Thought Replacement

At one time, we thought there was a single memory system in the brain. Thanks to recent advances in science and technology, we now know that memories are formed in a variety of systems and can easily be divided into two major categories:

Conscious Memory (i.e. explicit factual memory systems)

and

Unconscious or Subconscious Memory (i.e. **implicit emotional memory** systems)

We know that narcissists operate only in a world of explicit memory where emotions are non-existent. They have excellent explicit memory, which includes the details, the how to, when, where, and what of a situation or event. However, they have horrible implicit memory, which is always triggered by an emotion via a sense of smell, touch, taste, etc. As discussed earlier, narcissists are incapable of bringing forth emotional memories, only factual memories.

It is important to understand the difference between the two types of memory when trying to get over a narcissist. The reason is simple. Our emotional memory is extremely powerful and by learning how to harness its power, we can dramatically improve our quality of life.

We respond to events in our life based on images and memories we have stored in our subconscious. We can change how we respond to certain events in our life by engaging our subconscious. I believe our subconscious (i.e. emotional memory) drives all of our behavior. Therefore, learning how to tap into its power has amazing benefits.

To give you an idea of how powerful the subconscious is, compare it to the rate at which we speak. Our subconscious operates at a rate four times faster than we can speak. This is how we can multi-task, walk and chew gum at the same time. It is also how something we were trying to remember a few days ago suddenly pops into our head out of nowhere.

Have you ever forgotten someone's name or title of a movie? You can't think of it and tell yourself that you'll think of it later. When you do remember, it's while you're doing something completely unrelated. You weren't even thinking about it, but for some reason the name or title popped into your mind out of nowhere. Well, that is your subconscious mind at work. It never rests. It is always at work.

Psychologist, Joseph M. Carver Ph.D. helps us understand how *Emotional Memory Management* (EMM) enables us to manage our emotions in a way that will produce more POSITIVE outcomes for us. The key, of course, is managing how we RESPOND to our emotions.

We all know what memory is, but in the past we thought this memory simply contained data much like a computer maintains a system of files. New studies in psychology and neurology now tell us that the files not only contain data and information, but emotions as well. In a manner that is still not fully understood, our brain stores the emotions of an experience as they occurred at the time the memory was made.

As a result, memory files contain two parts: the information about the event and the feeling we had at the time the event occurred. Therefore, when we remember an event, we experience the same feelings we had at the time of the event. It is critical we understand how this impacts our behavior and the choices we make.

We experience a variety of emotions throughout a typical day. A specific area of the brain will hold memories for about five days. After this period, memories that are not important are typically erased and will never be recovered. A memory is important if it has a strong emotional impact on you and will hence be stored in your brain. Over time, we create a large file system of memories that consist of both positive and negative emotions.

Our brain pulls these memory files constantly without us even realizing it. According to Carver's research, our brain has the ability to pull memory files both on purpose and by accident. The good news here is that we can control what memory file we pull by selecting our thoughts. Perhaps even better news is the newfound knowledge that the brain only allows one emotional file out at a time.

According to Carver's research, the brain will focus on anything we choose, which means that we can choose which emotional file or tape we want to play. Even more significant, in my opinion, is the fact that the brain will only allow one emotional file or tape to play at a time. This means, if you decide to pull a different emotional file, your brain will completely go along with that idea.

Carver explains that the brain doesn't care which file is active. He compares it to breathing and explains that the brain operates in automatic just like when we breathe. It will automatically pull files throughout our day, just like breathing occurs without having to focus on it. However, in the same way that we can control our breathing by slowing down our inhale and exhale, we can also control our emotions by controlling what memory file we select.

When the brain operates in automatic, the files it pulls are influenced by our mood. Therefore, if you are depressed and your brain is on automatic, it will pull negative files that reinforce this mood. The key finding in this research is the discovery that we have the ability to change our mood or attitude by choosing which emotional file we pull.

As my best friend and very wise mother always says:

"Make it a great day or not. The choice is yours!"

She raised a happy family and founded a successful elementary school on this wonderful mantra, influencing generations of future students.

Realizing that we can influence our quality of life by choosing how we RESPOND to the things that happen to us is a huge discovery. It proves we really do have a choice.

Based on this research, I believe if you use the formula below when you are obsessing about your narcissist or stuck in a pattern of negative thinking, it will help you move on to more productive and healthy thoughts.

Negative Emotional Memory File is Pulled...

~ Causing you to think of your narcissist and potentially get stuck in a negative thinking pattern

Stop!

Replace with Positive Emotional Memory File...

~ Enabling you to replace the negative thinking with positive thinking and move on to more productive behavior

<u>Positive Thinking</u>

The power of positive thinking is huge. We have heard it all before, but I would like to expand on why I believe this to be true. I'm sure you have heard the saying, "We are what we eat," right? Well, I also believe that "we are what we think." If we choose to think positive thoughts, our lives will evolve accordingly. If we choose to think negative thoughts, a cycle of negativity will result.

It is critical that you understand you have the ability to influence the direction of your thoughts. I view depression as anger turned inward, which is a direct result of years of uninterrupted negative thinking patterns. The key is to INTERRUPT the negative patterns of thinking by replacing them with positive thoughts. Sounds pretty simple, doesn't it? Well, it is, but it does take time and dedication.

Depression develops over time so it may go without saying that it can take the same amount of time to recover from depression and break the pattern of negative thinking. The brain can heal itself after trauma, but it requires time. You can break the negative patterns of thinking by forcing your brain to strengthen other areas of your brain that are not related to memories of your toxic relationship.

If we think positively, endorphins and other pleasure-related substances are released, which strengthens a positive feedback cycle of thought, rather than negative. In this way, we do have the power to retrain our brain.

The knowledge that we can restore our brain's capacity to engage in healthy thinking patterns again is very reassuring. We must remember that anxiety is something we all experience. We cannot avoid it. It is part of the human condition. The key is learning how to RESPOND to anxiety.

"Learn to select your thoughts the same way you select your clothes every day. Now that's a power that you can cultivate."
~ Richard in "Eat, Pray & Love

Doing something positive to manage anxiety is a healthy coping strategy. Trying to feel better by drinking alcohol, dwelling in negativity or hoping anxiety or depression will simply go away will only lead to worsening symptoms. Practicing different methods of relaxation is an effective means of managing anxiety. Listed below are additional ways we can retrain our body and mind to respond to anxiety in a manner that is healthy and productive.

Create

One way to break negative patterns of thinking is to create something or start a new hobby. The more challenging the better because you want to occupy more resources in your brain towards learning something new rather than thinking about the past. When you are not actively thinking about your narcissist, the neuronal networks in your brain related to negative memories are not being strengthened. We can alter our own thought processes by using very simple methods and exercises.

Creativity allows us to express our emotions in a way nothing else can. Now that you no longer avoid feeling, start to celebrate the power of your emotions by expressing yourself creatively.

Dr. Stephen Diamond says creativity "is one of humankind's healthiest inclinations, one of our greatest attributes," and explains that our impulse to be creative "can be understood to some degree as the subjective struggle to give form, structure and constructive expression to inner and outer chaos and conflict."

Create your own prescription for promoting happiness. Whether you write poetry, paint, make pottery and crafts, knit, choreograph a dance, perform in a play, compose a song or simply put pen to paper to write something, to create makes us feel good!

Exercise

Exercise has been linked to positive mental health in numerous studies. Physically, exercise ' releases feel-good brain chemicals (neurotransmitters and endorphins) that ease depression and lift our overall mood. Exercise reduces immune system chemicals that can worsen depression. It increases our body temperature, which has a calming effect.

Next time you're feeling anxiety, cope in a healthy way and choose to respond by working out and getting physically active. Research on anxiety tells us that the physical and psychological benefits of exercise can help reduce anxiety and improve mood.

Psychologically, exercise helps you gain confidence by challenging you to meet goals. Getting in shape makes you feel better about your appearance. Working out is a wonderful distraction that can get you away from the cycle of negative thoughts that feed anxiety and depression.

By exercising, you can take your mind off your worries and give yourself time to think about how to respond to anxiety in the most productive manner. Remember, we all experience anxiety. The key is learning how to RESPOND to it. Exercise can also help anxiety and depression from coming back once you're feeling better.

I can personally testify to the fact that working out can help you relax and feel better. I find kick-boxing to be a wonderful outlet for stress and aggression. I'm addicted to the endorphin-rush of working out. It has an enormous positive effect on my psyche.

Music

Whether I play it, sing along or dance to it, music is like food for my soul. One of the best ways I have found to stop my brain from getting stuck in negative patterns of thinking is to turn on or play my favorite music.

"Music is the movement of sound to reach the soul for the education of its virtue. ~ Plato

The type of music that helps one person relax may be completely different from what helps another person relax. Whatever your preference, research shows that music significantly reduces anxiety and nervous system arousal.[4]

The body responds to rhythmic, soothing movement. This is why yoga has become such a popular form of exercise and explains why people enjoy dancing so much. Moving your body to a beat is extremely calming and enjoyable.

"In music the passions enjoy themselves." ~ Friedrich Nietzsche

I spent the winter of 2009 cutting an album with the *MHB Band* in a studio in Bucktown here in Chicago. I recorded 10 cover songs by my favorite female vocalists and one song I co-wrote with William Ellis and

Robin Grant of Nashville. Without a doubt, it was the most cathartic experience of my life. I created a tribute to it and the people who helped me create it at **www.GottaGetItOut.com** and will always cherish it.

I have a piece of artwork above my piano in my home that reads "Music is What Feelings Sound Like." Have you ever started crying when you heard a song that reminds you of someone from your past? That's your subconscious. The subconscious is where all of our emotion and creativity is stored, but we rarely tap into it. Often times, we avoid it. I believe if we harness the power of our subconscious we can help manifest our dreams to create a better life for ourselves. Music is the most effective and enjoyable outlet that allows me to do this. I highly encourage you to explore it as a means for expressing and ultimately finding your inner voice.

Breathing Techniques

"There are over two thousand organs and hormones that can be affected positively or negatively in a manner of minutes by shifting your breathing patterns," states Dr. Frank Lawlis, author of "Retraining the Brain." I'm sure you have heard that taking quick shallow breaths increases your anxiety. The reason for this is because short breaths signal to the brain that a threat exists, which automatically stimulates a stress response that leads to destructive patterns of thinking. On the other hand, taking deep breaths tells your brain all is well and allows you to relax.

One model of breathing I have found to be very effective when responding to anxiety is what Dr. Lawlis refers to as *Circle Breath*. The

idea is to keep a steady exchange of air inhaling and exhaling, creating a circle of airflow through the lungs. This should be done in a relaxed manner utilizing imagery. When inhaling, you should imagine positive and nurturing air entering your body and mind. While exhaling, you should think about releasing all the inner toxins and negative patterns of thinking into the air. Essentially, you are inhaling positive vibrations while exhaling toxic energy. [5]

Meditation

Meditation has been practiced since ancient times as a component of numerous religious traditions and has recently gained a great deal of empirical evidence to support its effectiveness.

According to Wikipedia, "Over 1000 published research studies support the fact that various methods of meditation have been linked to changes in metabolism, blood pressure, brain activation, and other bodily processes. Meditation has been used in clinical settings as a method of stress and pain reduction."

The aim of meditation is to bring inner peace within our self by changing our thoughts from negative to positive. By focusing within our self and tapping into our spirituality, we learn to transform and nurture the natural qualities within. Meditation is a self-healing process. The person who meditates gains a wonderful sense of their true self.

There are numerous styles of meditation practice. Since everyone responds to methods of meditation differently, I will not attempt to prescribe one technique over another. However, I highly recommend finding a form of meditation that works for you.

Meditation allows your mind to settle inward beyond thought to experience the source of thought – known as true consciousness, mindfulness or pure awareness. In this state, we are most in touch with our innermost self and feel most at peace.

"Within you there is a stillness and a sanctuary to which you can retreat at any time and be yourself." ~ Hermann Hesse

During meditation, we must allow ourselves to simply be and not fill in the space with outside noise or distraction. We must learn not to impulsively fill the empty space with our usual compulsions. Learning how to meditate is truly transformative for when we have seen ourselves completely, we no longer get jumpy or restless or need to keep busy. A thoroughly good relationship with oneself results in being able to be still in silence.

Massage

Our bodies are hardwired to need touch, but I don't recommend jumping into a new romantic relationship right away. You need to take time for yourself to heal. Therefore, get a massage from a professional or buy something you can use to massage yourself. The act of touch and massage releases endorphins and neurotransmitters like serotonin making you feel better physically and emotionally. Treat yourself to a massage or hot bath. You will be amazed at how much it relaxes you and reduces your anxiety.

Connect with Others

I believe we are all inter-connected. It is especially important during recovery to reach out to others. We only hurt ourselves when we disconnect or withdraw. Humans cannot thrive in isolation. When we connect with others we discover our kinship with one another. We realize we are not alone and others can relate to our pain. Our struggle seems less insurmountable because we have others who understand what we're going through. Talking to others who can relate is the best form of therapy I have ever found, which is precisely why I created our on-line forum at **www.ThePathForwardNow.com**.

Give Back to Others

Helping others is rewarding and fulfilling. I am dedicated to building awareness on the devastating effects of being in a relationship with a narcissist. It gives my life purpose and meaning. There are many ways to give back and help others, and I encourage you to do so as you grow stronger in your recovery.

"Experience is not what happens to you. It is what you do with what happens to you. Don't waste your pain; use it to help others." ~ Rick Warren

Celebrate Your Success

Positive reinforcement is necessary in order to implement any long-term change. Thanks to science we now know that retraining the brain is possible, but keep in mind the brain must experience positive reinforcement in order to fully integrate any significant change. We must enjoy what we are doing in order to continue doing it. If one coping strategy does not work for you, do not force yourself to continue it. Try another method. Everyone is different and what works for one person may not work for someone else. Keep trying until you find a strategy that you truly enjoy and can embrace. Celebrate success at every opportunity. Positive reinforcement must occur if any of these changes are going to last.

There is no overnight cure to repairing the damage caused by long-term emotional abuse and trauma in a relationship. If anyone tells you otherwise, please be cautious. In my opinion, any program that promises to fix you overnight or in a few quick sessions is exploiting victims. The key to any learning is repetition, time, practice and steadfast commitment.

The power to change is yours and yours alone. No one can take this gift from you, but you must treat it as a gift. Never take it for granted. Harness it and take control of this miraculous power you possess.

Learning how to cope with anxiety in a healthy way will allow you to start living and feeling again. Believe me when I tell you, I am living proof that it is possible to retrain your brain so you can stop negative obsessive patterns of thinking and start living life.

CHAPTER 6

STEP SIX
HEAL

We have a newfound compassion for ourselves and commit to live in the moment.

We must lighten up, relax and go easy on ourselves. Many of us find it easy to have compassion for others, but have very little for ourselves. It never occurs to us to feel it for ourselves. Living life with an unconditional love for ourselves changes everything. We get rid of the "should haves" and the "could haves" and gradually discover ourselves by being honest and staying in the moment. Without any agenda except for being real, we begin to find ourselves again. We assume responsibility for being here in this messy world and realize how precious life is.

I am often asked when the grieving ends. Everyone is different. You can't put a time frame on the healing process. What I do know is that the longer you avoid your pain, the longer it takes to recover. We must confront our pain and process it in order to heal and move on. As we discussed, writing about it helps, expressing ourselves helps, meditating helps. All of these things help, but it is up to you to put these things in motion for yourself. No one else can do it for you and until you do, you will remain stuck. You will not thrive. It is your choice.

By learning from the moments in life, we become more compassionate and can aspire to live in the now. We can relax and open our heart and mind to what is right in front of us in the moment. We see, feel and experience everything more vividly. This is living. Now is the time to experience enlightenment. Not some time in the future. Keep in mind, how we relate to the now creates the future.

"Nothing we can do can change the past, but everything we do changes the future." ~ Ashleigh Brilliant

134

When we find ourselves in a mess, we don't have to feel guilty about it and angry. Instead, we should reflect on the fact that how we RESPOND to the situation determines whatever happens next for us. We can become depressed and cynical or we can look at it as an opportunity to make ourselves strong. It is all a choice. Being brave enough to be fully alive and awake every moment of life, including the dark times, is to truly experience life to its fullest. What seems undesirable in life should not put us to sleep or deaden us. Instead, it should wake us up and remind us of the things we should appreciate.

The only true path to enlightenment is to drop all inner resistance and be honest. We must be true to ourselves. We must allow ourselves to feel our feelings and not be ashamed or afraid. In my opinion, all of our anxiety in life comes from:

REGRETTING THE PAST

or

WORRYING ABOUT THE FUTURE

Eckhart Tolle explains that each of us has a voice in our head that reminds us of troubles from our past and also encourages us to worry about our future. Some individuals listen to this voice more than others. Certain events or experiences can cause this voice in our head to run incessantly. *Cognitive Dissonance* is an example of this happening as a direct result of the emotional abuse we suffered.

Tolle helps us understand that all negativity is caused by too much focus on the past or future. He explains that worry and anxiety are caused by too much future focus and not enough presence. Being stuck in the past, either feeling resentful or guilty, is a result of too much past and not enough presence. By focusing on the past or future and denying the reality of your present, you remain stuck. Identification with your mind causes thought to be compulsive. Tolle explains that this mental noise prevents you from finding the realm of inner stillness inside you that is necessary to achieve enlightenment. [1]

Forgiveness Letter

It is critical that you have self-compassion for yourself right now in order to heal. Before you do anything else, it is important that you write a letter to yourself releasing you from any feelings of guilt you have for the toxic relationship you were in. We must forgive ourselves entirely for any part we played in continuing the relationship we had with an emotionally abusive person.

Your next writing assignment is crucial to your healing. You should now write a *Forgiveness Letter* to yourself for anything you are feeling guilty about because until you do this, you will remain stuck. You have done nothing wrong, but believe in the goodness of another person. Please do not beat yourself up for a poor choice, but instead forgive yourself and use the knowledge gained to never allow it to happen again.

Live in the Moment

Since the beginning of time, spiritual teachers of all traditions have pointed to the *Now* as the key to enlightenment. Meditation is one way you can learn to live in the moment and I highly recommend you explore it. It takes time to learn to stay focused on the present, and you may need to try more than one method before finding one that works for you, but please don't give up. It is easy to get distracted by time, noise, anxiety and fear. However, learning how to live in the moment is worth every bit of effort. Once you know how to do it, it is truly life-changing.

Eckhart Tolle points out that in life threatening situations, the shift to living in the moment happens naturally. The personality that is time-bound is replaced by an intense conscious presence that feels incredibly alive. Tolle says this is why some people enjoy engaging in dangerous activities, such as mountain climbing or skydiving. [2]

It makes sense. They may not be aware of it, but dangerous activities force you to live in the present. In a life or death situation, you must stay 100% focused on the present moment in order to ensure your survival. Slipping away from the present for even a second could prove deadly. This feeling of living in the moment reminds you that you are alive. It is intoxicating.

Travel

While it may not be easy at first, we can learn to enjoy the present moment and live life to its fullest by accepting that we are on a journey into the unknown. Instead of being afraid, let this inspire you!

Life should be a journey...an adventure. Travel is a wonderful way to get in touch with yourself. About five years ago, I spent 19 days traveling the Greek Islands. It was amazing to me how getting away from the noise of the city and my every day routine while journaling helped me find myself. It was truly a transformative experience I will never forget.

Live each day as if it were your last and cherish every moment of it. Learn to live with uncertainty for this is the first step on the spiritual path of awakening.

"Make Voyages. Attempt them. There's nothing else."
~ *Tennessee Williams*

Gratitude List

It is easy to forget the many blessings we have, which is why I encourage you to create a *Gratitude List* in your *Recovery Journal*. In this journal, you should write down everything you are grateful for in your life. Whenever you think of a new gratitude, add it to your journal. By writing this down, you will begin to see how truly blessed you are and appreciate the abundance in your life.

The present truly is a gift to be cherished. An *attitude of gratitude* can change your life. If you stop in the moment and ask yourself if you're ok, you realize you are not starving, you are not oppressed and you are not a prisoner of war somewhere. You are in a safe place and have much to be grateful for in life.

One of the best ways to learn to live in the moment is to stop allowing yourself to regret the past or worry about the future. This little saying helps me re-focus when I find myself struggling to stay in the moment:

Yesterday is History

Tomorrow, a Mystery

Today is a Gift

That's why it's called

The Present

Savor the Simplicities

It is a daily conscious effort to stay in the moment, especially in today's busy world. Appreciating the simple things in life is a good lesson for those who need to learn to live in the moment. By doing this, we begin to engage our senses to the point where everything we experience becomes more real and vivid. When we sense everything around us, we start to feel life.

This is when we begin to ENGAGE in life rather than merely OBSERVE it.

This is living!

Become fascinated with nature. The beauty of nature is one way God shows us he exists. Beauty provides us with a source of inspiration that is available everywhere to everyone. Embrace the gift of the present moment and realize how blessed you are. The present moment is all we really have.

The present should be the primary focus of your life. You can always cope with the present moment. However, you cannot cope with something that hasn't happened yet and you cannot change the past. You can control how you respond to the present moment, and how you respond to the present moment determines your future. We have a choice to be happy and embrace the moment or be miserable and remain stuck. I choose to be happy and hope you will join me in my journey.

Have a Love Affair with Yourself

If you're reading this book, you are most likely an *Empath*, which we discussed earlier. This means you have an intense feeling of empathy and compassion for others and it makes you feel good to take care of others. However, please do not rush into another relationship because of this instinct. Instead, channel it inward towards yourself. You need to take care of yourself for a change. You need to practice *Self-Compassion*!

Although taking care of yourself will feel foreign at first, it is the best thing you can do for yourself right now. It is critical for you to spend time alone before jumping into a new relationship. You need to find yourself again. You should not rush into a new relationship. You need to enjoy the benefits of being alone. You owe it to yourself.

We spend way too much time trying to form and nurture relationships with others who could potentially be our soul mate, when the whole time we neglect to nurture and get to know ourselves! It is time to have a love affair with yourself!

"To love oneself is the beginning of a life-long romance."
~ Oscar Wilde

You are finally living in the light and moving away from the darkness. It is time to connect with yourself again! Being in touch with yourself and your true emotions is truly a gift that we all must cherish and embrace.

As Sinead O'Connor says in one of my favorite songs:

"Feels So Different"

The whole time I'd never seen

All you had spread before me

The whole time I'd never seen

That all I'd need was inside me

Now I feel so different
I feel so different
I feel so different

It is time for you to realize all you need is inside yourself! It is time for you to have a love affair with yourself! You deserve it!

The Hidden Benefits of Struggle

As he says in his famous book "Man's Search for Meaning":

"Suffering ceases to be suffering the moment it finds a meaning." ~ Victor Frankl

This couldn't be more true, in my opinion. I know that had I not experienced what I did, I would not know myself the way I do now. Had certain events not forced me to look deep inside myself for strength, I would still be sleeping through life.

We must use everything that happens to us as a means for waking up. No one should feel shame for hard times. Suffering is a part of life. It is part of the human condition. The sooner we accept this, the better.

Stop avoiding pain and seeking only pleasure. Instead, start discovering the fundamental meaning behind the things we experience. I love what Frankl says here:

"We can discover meaning in life in three different ways: (1) by

creating a work or doing a deed; (2) by experiencing something or encountering someone; and (3) by the attitude we take toward unavoidable suffering." ~ Victor Frankl

Struggle toughens the human spirit and strengthens our character. It gives us purpose and direction. Following the path of least resistance in life is a cop-out. It is struggle and pain that leads to transformation.

This idea has changed many people's attitude towards suffering and I hope it changes yours as well. As you experience the pain of losing your narcissist, use it to empower you to discover the real meaning behind your relationship. I truly believe every relationship is meant to teach us something in life. Think about what you learned from this relationship. Things can be better for you not despite your suffering but because of it!

Moving Forward

"What doesn't kill us makes us stronger." ~ Friedrich Nietzsche

This has certainly been the case for me. I finally surrendered. What did I surrender? My ego. I stopped lying to myself that everything was ok. I dropped all inner resistance and started being honest with myself. I feel a sense of inner peace now that I never knew was possible.

To live in denial and avoidance is to prefer death over life. Others may have lied to us for years, but to lie to ourselves is no longer acceptable. It is no way to live. You can't run from yourself, avoid your feelings, or deny your reality for any longer. No one who is lying to themselves is living in the light of consciousness. Enlightenment is what we all seek, but in order to achieve this, we first must be honest with ourselves about our situation. We cannot avoid anger and fear. We must feel these feelings, confront them and process them before we can truly

142

move on.

We should never be afraid to ask for support from others in our quest to evolve. I believe we are all interconnected. If we need to heal, we must reach out to others. If you have learned anything from my story, I hope you have learned that people only hurt themselves when they disconnect or withdraw from others. Being afraid to ask for help only leads to further isolation. Humans cannot thrive in isolation. Do not endure this alone. Reach out to a family member, friend, mental health professional or visit our on-line forum at www.ThePathForwardNow.com. You are never alone.

Please do not close yourself off from others because you have been hurt. You were born giving and receiving love and you are still capable of loving in every way that is humanly possible. Embrace your ability to feel love and compassion. It truly is a gift.

"Eventually you will come to understand that love heals everything, and love is all there is." ~ *Gary Zukav*

As I mentioned, I am not a religious person, but I am very spiritual. I believe in a higher power, a higher energy that makes the sun come up every day. It is our responsibility to tap into that energy that exists within us. We all possess the energy to make the sun come up in our lives every day.

When we stop lying to ourselves, accept what we can and cannot control and begin living in the moment, we finally start to live in a state of consciousness that will bring us happiness. It is that simple. It may sound complicated, but it really is not.

Every day is a gift and every day we wake up, we have a choice. A choice about whether we want to tap into our positive energy or wallow in negative energy. Happiness is a choice we all have. Remember, it is not about what happens to us. It is about how we RESPOND to life that matters.

I leave you with one of my favorite quotes:

"When I was five years old, my mom told me that happiness was the key to life. When I went to school, they asked me what I wanted to be when I grew up. I wrote down "happy." They told me I didn't understand the assignment. I told them they didn't understand life." ~ John Lennon

You hold the power within to cultivate a life of happiness for yourself, but it is up to you to take control and make that happen. It is my hope that *The Path Forward* will provide a path for you to take back control of your life, find yourself again and manifest your dreams. Tap into your innate potential.

A whole new world is out there waiting for you.

Embrace it because <u>YOU</u> deserve it!

Summary of Writing Assignments

Share Your Story

Letter to the Narcissist

Letter from the Narcissist

What I will Not Forget List

What I Can Control vs. What I Cannot Control

Forgiveness Letter

Gratitude List

Notes

Introduction

1. Jean M. Twenge and W. Keith Campbell, "The Narcissism Epidemic – Living in the Age of Entitlement" (New York: Free Press/Simon &Schuster, 2009).

Chapter 1

1. Sam Vaknin, "Malignant Self-Love – Narcissism Revisited" (Prague: Narcissus Publications, 2006).
2. Ibid.
3. Ibid.
4. Ibid.

Chapter 3

1. Louise DeSalvo, "Writing as Way of Healing – How Telling Our Stories Transforms Our Lives" (Boston: Beacon Press, 1999), p. 43.
2. Eckhart Tolle, "The Power of Now" (Vancouver, BC: Namestate Publishing, 1999).

Chapter 5

1. Dr. Frank Lawlis, *Retraining the Brain* (New York: Penguin Books, 2009).
2. Fred Penzel, *Obsessive-Compulsive Disorders* (New York: Oxford University Press, 2000).
3. Lawlis, *Retraining the Brain.*
4. Ibid.
5. Ibid.

Chapter 6

1. Eckhart Tolle, *The Power of Now* (Vancouver, BC: Namestate Publishing, 1999).
2. Ibid.

About the Author

Lisa E. Scott wrote her first book "It's All About Him" to help women recognize the harmful effects of being in a relationship with a narcissist. "Surviving a Narcissist" is her second book, which she hopes will provide a Path Forward to those recovering from the emotional abuse that occurs in a relationship with a narcissist.

Ms. Scott is a native of the Chicagoland area who resides downtown in the heart of historic Printer's Row. She is an Adjunct Professor at Loyola University Chicago where she teaches Organizational Behavior and is also a Human Resources representative for a global professional services firm.

THE PATH FORWARD COACHING

Immediate Help with Expert Advice!

One-on-One Consultation applying "The Six Steps of The Path Forward"
to help you move on after an emotionally abusive relationship."

• Talk to an Expert, Privately by Phone, One-on-One

- Ask the questions **that you need answers** to RIGHT NOW and **apply to YOUR particular situation**.

- Help you to **eliminate the narcissist and negative people** from your life, **once and for all!**

• Improve the DAILY Quality of YOUR Life

- For your kids (if you have them), your family members, and **most of all, YOU!**

- Even just one phone session with one of our **Relationship Coaches** can help save you from all the daily frustrations and challenges that come with getting over a toxic relationship.

- **Eliminate the relationship problems** you just don't know how to fix on your own.

• Start Experiencing More Enjoyable and Fulfilling Days

- After all, **YOU** are the only one who can put in motion the change you want to see in your life. Relationship Coaching gives you the capacity and energy you need to get through the day more enjoyably and create a life of happiness for yourself.

- Loving and caring Support to move on AND **find a new healthy vibrant relationship for yourself, which is what you deserve!**

"The Path Forward" Relationship Coaching gives you the support,
confidence and roadmap you need to finally move on,
find yourself again and reclaim your life.

Take the first step to improving the quality of your life TODAY!

148